Genes and Insurance
Ethical, Legal and Economic Issues

The results are examined here of two key social developments in recent years: the partial dismantling of the welfare state and the progress of genetics. Genetic insights are becoming increasingly valuable for risk assessment, and insurers would like to use these insights to help determine premiums. Combined with the fact that social welfare is being curtailed, this could potentially create an uninsured high-risk population. Along with considerations of autonomy and privacy, this forms the basis for an ethical critique of insurers' access to information. There has often been regulation of such information, but the authors argue that because of adverse selection regulation will not solve these problems and may jeopardise the survival of private personal insurance. Instead, we should look towards the resurrection of social insurance, a key component of the welfare state. This book will interest academic researchers and professionals involved with genetics and insurance.

MARCUS RADETZKI is Research Fellow in Private Law in the Faculty of Law, Stockholm University, and Assistant Professor in Private Law in the Department of Law, Örebro University. His recent publications include 'Limitation of Third Party Nuclear Liability: Causes, Implications and Future Possibilities' (*Nuclear Law Bulletin*, 1999) and 'Cause and Damage – Interpretation of Liability-Activating Terms in Property Insurance' (*Scandinavian Studies in Law*, 2000).

MARIAN RADETZKI is Professor in the Department of Economics, Luleå University of Technology, and a Senior Research Fellow at Studieförbundet Näringsliv och Samhälle (Centre for Business and Policy Studies), a Stockholm think tank. His recent publications include *Fashions in the Treatment of Package Waste: An Economic Analysis of the Swedish Producer Responsibility Legislation* (2000) and *The Green Myth: Economic Growth and the Quality of the Environment* (2001).

NIKLAS JUTH is a Lecturer in the Institute of Philosophy, Göteborg University. His publications include 'När är idrotten jämställd?' ('When Shall We Have Equity in Sports?', *Filosofisk tidskrift*, 2000) and 'Insurance Companies' Access to Genetic Information: Why Regulation Alone Is Not Enough' (*Monash Bioethics Review*, 2003).

i

Cambridge Law, Medicine and Ethics

This is a series of books focusing on medical law, but including titles in which both legal and ethical policy issues are discussed. The series is intended to respond to the growing importance of medical law not only in universities and in legal and medical practice, but in public and political affairs. It aims to reflect the fact that many major policy issues over the last few years have had a strong medical law dimension (organ retention, embryonic stem cell research, safety issues etc.). The emphasis is therefore on issues of public concern or practical significance rather than merely on the theoretical dimensions of the subject.

General Editor
Professor Alexander McCall Smith

Editorial Advisory Board
Dr Alexander Morgan Capron, *Director, Ethics and Health, World Health Organization*
Professor Jim Childress, *University of Virginia*
Professor Margot Brazier, *University of Manchester*
Dr Ruth Chadwick, *University of Lancaster*
Dame Ruth Deech, *University of Oxford*
Professor Martin Bobrow, *University of Cambridge*

Marcus Radetzki, Marian Radetzki, Niklas Juth
Genes and Insurance: Ethical, Legal and Economic Issues
0 521 83090 7

Ruth Macklin, *Biomedical Research in Developing Countries: Double Standards*
0 521 83388 4 hardback   0 521 54170 0 paperback

Genes and Insurance

Ethical, Legal and Economic Issues

Marcus Radetzki
Marian Radetzki
Niklas Juth

CAMBRIDGE
UNIVERSITY PRESS

PUBLISHED BY THE PRESS SYNDICATE OF THE UNIVERSITY OF CAMBRIDGE
The Pitt Building, Trumpington Street, Cambridge CB2 1RP, United Kingdom

CAMBRIDGE UNIVERSITY PRESS
The Edinburgh Building, Cambridge, CB2 2RU, UK
40 West 20th Street, New York, NY 10011–4211, USA
477 Williamstown Road, Port Melbourne, VIC 3207, Australia
Ruiz de Alarcón 13, 28014 Madrid, Spain
Dock House, The Waterfront, Cape Town 8001, South Africa

http://www.cambridge.org

First published in Swedish by SNS Förlag as *Att nyttja genetisk
information* 2002 and © Forfattarna och SNS Förlag 2002.
This updated edition first published in English by
Cambridge University Press 2003

Printed in the United Kingdom at the University Press, Cambridge

Typeface Plantin 10/12 pt.   *System* LATEX 2ε   [TB]

A catalogue record for this book is available from the British Library

ISBN 0 521 83090 7 hardback

Contents

Preface

The ideas contained in this book matured gradually over a period of some two years at the end of the 1990s in discussions between Marcus Radetzki and Marian Radetzki. A minor grant from the Trygg Hansa Research Foundation early in 2000 made it possible to start work in a small way. The result was a paper in Swedish, 'Genetic Knowledge and Insurance', by Marcus Radetzki, published in *Nordisk Försäkringstidskrift (Scandinavian Insurance Quarterly)* in 2001. The paper provides an overview of the subject area, and constituted a starting point for the present work. At a later stage during preparations, Niklas Juth was associated with the team, with the special task of covering the ethical aspects arising from the issues under investigation.

Work on the book was undertaken during the period September 2001–September 2002, with Studieförbundet Näringsliv och Samhälle (SNS – a Swedish think tank) as an administrative base, and a Swedish edition was published by SNS during 2002.

The manuscript is the result of close collaboration between the authors, but the work has been divided according to the authors' areas of competence. Chapters 1 and 8 have been jointly written by Marcus Radetzki and Marian Radetzki. Niklas Juth carried the main responsibility for chapters 2 and 7 and Marcus Radetzki for chapters 3 and 6, while Marian Radetzki wrote chapters 4 and 5.

While the responsibility for remaining weaknesses and errors rests entirely with the authors, we wish to acknowledge and thank for their valuable and highly constructive comments on earlier versions of the manuscript Göran Flood (insurance specialist), Christian Munthe (philosopher) and Jan Wahlström (geneticist), and three anonymous referees appointed by Cambridge University Press. Teresa Bjelkhagen and Timothy Chamberlain have provided valuable help in making sense of the English language, not our mother tongue. Generous grants from ELSA, the Swedish research programme, from Sven and Dagmar Salén's Research Foundation and from Swedish Ethics in Health Care have been crucial prerequisites for the work. We express our sincere thanks and hope that the results of our effort are up to our benefactors' expectations.

MARCUS RADETZKI, MARIAN RADETZKI and NIKLAS JUTH
Stockholm, December 2002

1 Introduction

This book is about the confluence of two developments which assumed significance during the 1990s in most rich market economies on both sides of the Atlantic. Unexpected consequences followed the combination of the two tendencies, and they led to a set of political decisions which, on closer scrutiny, appear to be neither well founded nor sustainable.

The first development is the remarkable progress made in genetics during the 1990s and the promise of even greater potential gains in the not-too-distant future. In the 1990s it became possible to identify the relationship between defective genes and a set of serious illnesses. This insight strengthened the incentives to develop genetic testing which could potentially anticipate many more illnesses, as well as therapies to reduce the risk of the illnesseses breaking out or to provide remedies once they have done so. The number of illnesses that can be prognosticated or diagnosed with the help of genetics is steadily growing. In consequence, genetic insights become increasingly more valuable as instruments for assessing the risk of illness as well as longevity. In a somewhat longer time perspective, there are clear possibilities for the use of genetics to reduce the outbreak of illnesses with genetic origin, and to limit the risk of such illnesses. In an even longer perspective, this new branch of science appears to offer the potential to manipulate genes not only to avoid illness but to improve individual characteristics and qualities in various respects. In the very long run, genetic knowledge is thought to have the potential for creating a new species, a 'superhuman', but such speculation is currently part of science fiction rather than science.

The second development is a contemporaneous transformation of the social insurance systems that were built up during the first half of the twentieth century, and consolidated in its third quarter, in the welfare states around the north Atlantic. The evolution of social insurance has taken somewhat different paths in the countries under review (see chapter 4), but several key features have been common everywhere. Thus, the systems have all been motivated by solidarity, and characterized by strong collective and mandatory elements; public involvement has been complete in many cases and predominant in others, while the profit motive has been completely absent or strongly subdued. Social insurance has covered many aspects of life, but our interest is limited to those whose goals have been to insure against the cost of treatment in the event of illness, and against loss of income due to illness or premature death, or during old age. In the 1990s the systems of social insurance were subjected to a partial dismantling. The main reasons for this development are (i) the fast expansion of public financial obligations; (ii) a desire to make the provision of insurance services more efficient; and (iii) a wish to expand the freedom of choice of those insured, and so to facilitate the satisfaction of each individual's particular needs. The reforms of the 1990s have comprised (i) the partial individualisation and commercialisation of the public arrangements; (ii) a lesser generosity towards those insured; and (iii) an active encouragement to seek private supplements to the remaining public arrangements. The supply of private personal insurance by profit-making insurance companies operating in competitive markets has been strongly stimulated by these reforms.

The confluence of the two developments has created a set of new opportunities but also a number of fears. There was no need for individual risk assessments in the collective and mandatory social insurance systems. In contrast, the commercial insurance companies that have taken over in part from these systems desire, as far as possible, to adjust the premiums that they charge to their customers, and to place restraints on the extent of the service that they provide (in the case of health insurance), or to exclude the cover of certain causes of premature death, in accordance with the risk represented by each individual engagement. The emerging genetic technology provides a powerful instrument for individual risk assessments for the health, premature death and pension policies underwritten by private insurers. Access to such risk information will facilitate more precise actuarial premium assessments, and so make the insurance business more efficient. Uncertainty remains regarding the extent to which genetic science will be able to play such a role in risk assessment (chapter 2). To some extent it does so already, and therefore insurance companies feel a need to take genetic insights into account, just as they must seek and obtain all other information of relevance for assessing risk.

Simultaneously, the freedom of insurance companies to employ genetic insights in risk assessment is being increasingly questioned on ethical grounds. With reference to the individual's right to autonomy and privacy, it is claimed that he should be free to remain ignorant about possible defects in his genetic make-up and under no circumstances be coerced into handing over such intimate information to others. At a time when social insurance systems are being partially dismantled, arguments of solidarity and equality have also been a starting point for criticising the use of genetic information for the purpose of insurance. Genetic insights make it possible to widen the range of premiums charged for private personal insurance, and/or to vary the extent of cover for the treatment of an illness. The actuarial justice of each insured paying for the risk he represents, no more and no less, has been criticised and juxtaposed against the injustice that follows from a discriminatory situation where some are forced to pay more, or to accept a less comprehensive cover, because of a genetic make-up that is not of their own choice. Such a concept of injustice has been at the forefront of many public debates.

The criticism directed towards what has been perceived as injustice has resulted in restrictive regulation of insurance companies' access to genetic information. Clearly, the insurance industry in all countries is subject to a variety of regulatory regimes, but in what follows, attention is entirely focused on the regulation related to the access to and use of genetic information. In some countries, Austria, Belgium, Norway and Denmark among them (but also in a few states in the United States), regulation has been given the form of legislation. In other countries, for example the Netherlands, Sweden and the United Kingdom, regulation is in the form of an agreement between the government and insurers' associations, in which the insurance companies commit themselves not to use genetic information other than under particular specified circumstances. Since the problems related to genetic information and personal insurance are new and their practical importance is growing, it is our belief that regulation restricting insurance companies' access to genetic insights will be introduced in an increasing number of countries.

As noted, regulation can take the form of either legislation or a voluntary agreement. In chapter 3, where existing regulatory arrangements are described and analysed, we discuss this distinction in some detail. In the rest of the book, however, we find little reason to distinguish between the two forms. One could of course claim that agreements are less stable, since they can be cancelled when one of the parties so desires. However, since cancellation by the insurance industry can immediately be countered by legislation, the practical implications of the difference between the two regulatory forms appear to us to be insignificant.

The content of regulation, in contrast, requires a rough categorisation into two fundamental types. The first, called *partial regulation* in what follows, prevents insurance companies from requiring their clients to undertake genetic testing as a precondition for a policy, but allows them to demand access to information in already existing tests. The second, *total regulation*, prohibits the latter as well. Some countries that have so far introduced restrictions in this area have chosen total regulation. In other countries a mixture of the two is applied. Thus the insurance companies are prohibited from requiring new tests. Access to results from existing tests, however, is permitted when the insured amount exceeds a pre-specified amount.

The political decisions partially to dismantle existing social insurance systems may well have had strong and well-founded motivations. However, a consequence is that private personal insurance has in many cases become a basic good of overriding significance for social welfare. This is the background against which the proliferating restrictions against the insurance industry's use of genetic insights should be seen. Fundamental welfare goals must not be compromised through increased differentiation of insurance premiums, which could make insurance unaffordable for exposed groups, or through genetically motivated restrictions of cover that leave them unprotected altogether. Regulation can be seen in this light as an appropriate action, certainly in the short and medium run. However, it seems to us that the political decision-makers have not sufficiently considered the long-run consequences of the restrictions that they have introduced.

Private insurance companies play an important role in market-oriented economies. *Asymmetric information* and *adverse selection* are two related problems that always threaten to undermine the activities of profit-making insurance businesses that operate in competitive markets (Akerlof, 1970, pp. 480 ff.), and firms must always act to minimise both. The insurance companies have strong incentives to obtain information about their clients, and to charge a premium in each case that corresponds to the risk of that case. The insurers who fail in this task will make losses on policies that represent a high risk. At the same time there is a likelihood that clients representing low risks who are charged premiums in excess of this risk, will gradually switch to competing insurance companies prepared to offer them a lower, actuarially determined premium. Continuous analysis of risks and the adjustment of premiums or extent of cover to the cost represented by each risk are therefore preconditions for the long-term health of the private insurance company.

Genetic insights constitute an instrument for risk analysis in personal insurance. At the beginning of the twenty-first century the potential of genetics in this regard is not overwhelming, but it is growing rapidly. Prohibition of the use of genetic insights for insurance risk analysis might well contribute towards greater equality, but at the cost of lowered efficiency in the insurance business. The precise reasons why private insurance firms operating in competitive markets should assume the burden of equality promotion in this regard, and why *genetic* information should be banned as a premium differentiating tool, are neither self-evident nor clear.

The consequences of restricting regulation will be particularly serious for insurance companies when some of their competitors can avoid the restrictions through their location. Adverse selection will become an increasingly serious problem to the domestic insurance industry, as rising numbers of clients representing below-average risk move their business to insurance companies located offshore, which are not subject to regulation. Ultimately, regulation may impose a survival threat to the domestic insurance industry and by implication to the domestic supply of personal insurance. Regulation loses all justification if the ultimate outcome is the breakdown of the domestic insurance market.

From a legal perspective it is clear that existing restrictions on the use of genetic information for the purpose of insurance constitute part of a wider set of regulations to prevent discrimination in the private sector. Our analyses reveal that existing prohibitions of such discrimination are not based on uniform legal criteria in the countries under review. It would appear that rules against discrimination have been introduced from time to time independent of each other, and each time as a result of political fashion. Thus the existing restrictions against genetic discrimination in the field of insurance are not based on any uniform and consistent system of rules regarding discrimination in the private sector, because no such system is in existence. Since regulation to prevent genetic discrimination in the field of insurance has been set up without the application of any general and uniform legal principles, we conclude that it can also be abolished without reference to such principles.

We should also add that the ethical foundations of the regulation under scrutiny are far from clear-cut. Some ethical arguments provide an unambiguous support for the existing restrictions. But, as will be clear from our investigations, several other ethical considerations point in the opposite direction.

Fascinating combinations of genetic insights and insurers' interests can be envisaged in the longer run, to prevent illnesses or ameliorate their course by indicating early prophylactic interventions, so as to improve the life of the insured, and reduce the cost to the insurer. In the absence of regulation insurance companies will have strong incentives to contribute to the developments in genetics, so as to reduce the cost of genetic risks. Such developments are likely to be delayed, or could fail to materialise altogether, as a consequence of the regulations under review.

In sum, then, these observations lead us to the conclusion that the restrictions on insurance companies' use of genetic information are not sustainable and will be repealed. Important aspects of welfare will be hurt in consequence. In the last part of the book we discuss how the rich welfare states on both sides of the north Atlantic could act to resolve economic issues and at the same time protect the genetically exposed population groups from suffering.

The book is divided into four parts. Part I provides the main starting points for the analyses that follow. Chapter 2 is intended for the novice in the field of genetic science. We introduce basic genetic terms, and discuss how genetic science has evolved and its significance for the insurance industry. We also outline the likely role that this science may play in the future, especially as an instrument to assess risk. In chapter 3 we present the regulation that restrains the insurance industry's access to genetic information. We also review its motivations and implications for the insurance industry and its clients.

Part II deals with the social, economic and legal aspects of genetic knowledge and personal insurance. Chapter 4 provides a brief history of social insurance, from its emergence early in the twentieth century to its maturing after the Second World War, the emerging problems during the 1970s and 1980s, and the partial dismantling of the obligatory, collective arrangements in the 1990s. An important reason to doubt the sustainability of the regulation that restricts insurance companies' access to genetic information is explored in chapter 5. As the world economy becomes increasingly integrated, we expect a greatly expanded international trade in personal insurance. Since absence of regulation in this regard provides a clear-cut competitive edge, we anticipate a rising propensity to relocate insurance activities to countries where such restrictions do not apply. Insurance companies subject to regulation will then increasingly suffer from adverse selection, and in consequence gradually lose their share of the market. It is clear that such developments raise the likelihood of deregulation, and an ensuing freer access to genetic information for all insurance endeavours. We note, however, that some regulation is maintained even when its stated objectives are not achieved. One important reason why this is so is that it forms part of a broader regulatory system, and there is an unwillingness to break that system. In consequence, chapter 6 explores whether the regulation of the insurance industry's access to genetic information is in fact a coherent part of a broader, uniform regulatory system. The system that we investigate in this context relates to the legislation concerning discrimination in general in the private sector.

Part III treats the ethical issues arising from insurance companies' access to genetic information thus, chapter 7 discusses whether consequentialist arguments, reasons related to the individual's autonomy and privacy or outright justice can be seen to provide support for regulation. The most important consideration appears to be that personal insurance has developed into a basic good, of great importance for welfare. Consequently, the inability of groups with genetic deficiencies to obtain insurance because premiums become prohibitively expensive or because insurance companies refuse to offer insurance at any price, cannot be regarded as acceptable on ethical grounds.

Part IV summarises and develops further the analytical results of earlier parts. In chapter 8 we demonstrate that politicians have apparently not thought through the combined consequences of their decisions regarding the partial dismantling of social insurance, on the one hand, and restrictions against the use of genetic insights in personal insurance, on the other. Our most important conclusion is that the existing total regulation of the use of genetic information in the field of insurance should be abrogated. Such an action will undoubtedly arouse a variety of economic as well as social and ethical problems. The chapter discusses how to come to grips with these problems.

A few clarifications are needed before we conclude this introductory chapter. Our concept *personal insurance* comprises three different forms of insurance, namely (i) insurance against income loss and for the cost of treatment in the event of illness; (ii) insurance against income loss due to the premature death of a household's income earner; and (iii) insurance to provide income during old age. Our analysis is limited geographically to the fifteen member countries of the European Union, along with Norway and Switzerland, and to the United States and Canada on the other side of the Atlantic. As mentioned, we differentiate between two types of regulation of insurance companies' access to genetic information: *partial regulation* forbids insurance companies to demand that new tests be undertaken as a precondition for insurance, but allows them to demand information from tests that already exist; *total regulation* forbids the latter as well. Two concepts that are frequently used in the following chapters are *asymmetric information*, a circumstance where the insured knows more about the insured risk than the insurance company, and *adverse selection*, defined as a situation where the insured group comprises a declining number of low risks and a mounting number of high ones. We distinguish between the degree of risk represented by individuals. *Low risks* comprise insured individuals whose risk is lower than the average in the insured group, *high risks* are the insured individuals whose risks are higher than the same average. There is no other connotation in the concepts 'low' and 'high' in this context.

Part I

Starting points

2 The terminology and possibilities of genetics

2.1 Introduction[1]

Contemporary genetics has caused immense debate in ethics and the social sciences.[2] Some recent discussion has the feel of science fiction and concerns future possibilities for human cloning and alteration of the genome to eliminate diseases or maybe even improve human capacities, in so far as they are genetically determined. This debate has already prompted us to ponder possible future developments, but these often involve scenarios so uncertain that it cannot be determined today how credible their realisation might be.

This book about genetics and personal insurance is not concerned to any great extent with addressing hypothetical possibilities. The technology that is relevant to the debate already exists: genetic testing. Use is already being made of these tests in the health services of the developed countries to establish or further secure diagnoses and to estimate the risk attached to a wide range of diseases before onset.

It is the latter purpose of genetic testing that is of primary interest to insurance companies, that is testing for diseases that have not yet revealed any symptoms. Many serious genetically determined diseases affect the individual early on in life.[3] Since the symptoms appear early, these diseases will not be relevant in the following discussion. However, genetic testing can be used to predict the onset of some diseases that affect adults, or at least the risk of onset. At present, most of these diseases are very rare and very serious. There are various medical purposes for performing such tests, for example, in order to recommend changes in lifestyle or offer prophylactic treatment in order to prevent or reduce the risk of

---

[1] This chapter has gained tremendously from the expertise of the geneticist Jan Wahlström. All responsibility for the content and its flaws is the authors'.

[2] Harris, 1998, provides an accessible introduction to the ethical debate on the subject.

[3] For instance, Tay-Sach's disease and Lesch-Nyhan's syndrome (Connor and Ferguson-Smith, 1997, pp. 130 ff.).

the disease in question, or in order to develop biochemical treatment. Genetic testing of this type can also be used to identify carriers of genes that will not affect the carriers themselves, but which can cause disease or risk of disease to their children.

In the following section we will present a brief account of the science of genetics that has made genetic testing possible. The possibilities genetics offers for the future will be discussed in section 2.3, while we estimate the relevance of the increasing number of genetic insights to the private insurance industry in section 2.4. Before this we wish to counter a common but fundamental misunderstanding by emphasising the limits of genetic science.

The following claim is crucial in order to understand this chapter: *a gene in itself can never give rise to the properties of an individual and can only affect an individual given an environment.* Contrary to this claim, there is a widespread view that human nature is identical with, or determined by, the individual's genes. This view, presented in so loose a fashion, can of course be interpreted in several, more or less reasonable, ways. The view that a person's genes constitute his nature (or are central to it) is sometimes called genetic essentialism and the view that a person is a product solely of his genes is sometimes called genetic determinism (Launis, 2000, p. 309). We shall not uphold this distinction, but use the term genetic essentialism for both, since we reject both these views. As will be clear in what follows, modern genetics shows that these kinds of views are based on gross misunderstandings of the significance of biological inheritance. The environment is not something that becomes significant after the creation of the biological individual with all his characteristics. Environment is there from the start at all levels: the chemical and biological as well as the social, economic and cultural (moreover, the latter levels affect the former, for instance by the impact our technology has on nature). Environments thus always have a crucial significance for the characteristics of any individual. The biological individual is consequently a product of the interaction between genes and environment.

An example from the vegetable kingdom may be illuminating. In May two sunflower seeds with an identical genetic make-up are planted. One is planted in cultivated soil on the south side of the house, regularly watered and supported by a steady stick. The other is planted in the backyard, competing with weeds, fighting the wind and receiving water at irregular intervals from whatever rain may fall. By September the first plant has become an almost ten-foot high sunflower with a giant flower at the top, while the other barely reaches a foot above the ground and seems unlikely to bloom before the winter.

2.2 Some basic genetic terminology[4]

What is a gene? What kind of information is genetic information? How can this kind of information reveal anything about a person's susceptibility to certain diseases?

Genes have two main functions. They provide a mechanism for inheritance between generations and a mechanism for the development of the biological individual. The latter process can now be explained to an increasing extent.

All living organisms consist of *cells* (the genetic vocabulary in italics is collected and explained in table 2.1). Cells are biochemical systems that contain, among other things, a long molecule: its *DNA*. DNA, or deoxyribonucleic acid, is built up of a sugar phosphate backbone with nitrogenous bases (A, G, C and T), which, because of their chemical constructions, can be combined in varied but limited ways. A *gene* is a part of the DNA that, in the appropriate chemical environment, via RNA (ribonucleic acid), creates a protein – that is, this part of the DNA interacts chemically with its environment and the product of this interaction is a protein. This is in fact the definition of a gene: a unit of DNA, which codes for one specific protein. The proteins 'do the work' in the cell. Among other things, they decide the function of the cell, whether it is to be a heart cell, liver cell, nerve cell, and so on. The chemical process is complicated, and scientists are far from fully grasping it yet.

The general idea, however, is that the genes are a part of the construction of the *phenotype*, that is the individual.[5] This takes place through a number of steps: gene (DNA), RNA, protein, cell and so on. Each one of these steps is sensitive to influence from environmental factors and, sometimes, other genes. This means that the impact of a single gene on an individual is difficult to determine. Geneticists know more about the chemical construction of the DNA than they know about the impact of genes on the cell and even less about their impact on the whole organism (Buchanan *et al.*, 2000, p. 349).

Sometimes genes are randomly changed, as a result of external influence (for instance, radioactivity or foreign chemical substances) or because they fail to make an exact copy of themselves when the cell divides.

---

[4] This very rudimentary account of genetics is part of the standard view of the functioning of genes and the literature is of course vast. An accessible, while fairly detailed, account can be found in Connor and Ferguson-Smith, 1997.

[5] Sometimes the properties of the phenotype are defined as the properties that are directly perceptible. However, in modern biology, it is more of a 'dustbin category' which is used to refer to all the non-genetic properties of the biological individual, such as height, blood type, taste in music and so on (Buchanan *et al.*, 2000, p. 354).

Such a change in genes is called *mutation*. Sometimes mutations damage the genes permanently, damage that eventually causes disease.

Genetic disorders differ with regard to how many of those who carry the gene actually fall ill (*penetrance*) and how grave the symptoms are (*expressivity*). Some genes always give rise to specific symptoms and some only increase the risk that some of a variety of symptoms will emerge.

A gene consists of two parts or alleles, one inherited from the mother and one from the father. All genes are organised in chromosomes. Humans have forty-six chromosomes, twenty-three from each parent. The likelihood of receiving a given allele is 50 per cent. An allele can be *dominant* or *recessive*. If it is dominant, one allele alone is sufficient to contract the disease or the risk of the disease, that is you need only inherit the genetic abnormality from one parent. If the allele is recessive you have to inherit it from both parents. If you inherit a recessive genetic abnormality from one parent only, you are a healthy carrier of the genetic abnormality. This means that you can pass on the gene to your children, who may become ill if the other parent is also a carrier (the likelihood in this case is 25 per cent).[6] Some genetic diseases, such as haemophilia, are inherited through genes located on the sex chromosomes, so that the impact of the gene is determined by the person's sex (usually the gene is located on the X chromosome, so that males get the disease and females are healthy carriers).[7]

In medical and legal literature a distinction is often made between three kinds of genetic testing. *Presymptomatic genetic testing* aims at identifying a single gene disorder in order to predict whether the tested person will develop the disease or not (the genetic testing vocabulary in italics is collected and explained in table 2.2). Another kind of genetic testing tries to establish whether the tested person has an increased risk of developing certain diseases that are generally caused by a combination of environmental factors and a number of genes. This kind of genetic testing is called *predictive genetic testing*. Sometimes individuals are healthy carriers of genes which can be inherited by following generations and cause diseases there. Tests for these genes are called *genetic carrier detection*.

As indicated above, some genetic diseases or risks of diseases are *single gene disorders*, that is, they are the result of the abnormality of one particular gene. Examples of such diseases are some special forms of cancer, cystic fibrosis, Huntington's disease and sickle-cell anaemia. Short descriptions of two such diseases follow.

---

[6] The matter is complicated because of the phenomenon of 'crossing over', which splits up and combines chromosomes in arbitrary ways.

[7] Genes that are not located on the sex chromosome are called autosomal.

Table 2.1. *Explanations of some basic genetic terms*

Term	Explanation
cell	The building block of all living things, which includes the cell core containing DNA.
DNA	The chemical carrier of our inheritance. Short for deoxyribonucleic acid, a long molecule shaped like a spiral staircase, built up of sugar phosphate as the sides of the staircase, with nitrogenous bases acting as the steps.
RNA	Mediates the chemical 'message' from the DNA to the cell. Short for ribonucleic acid. Consists of one side of a DNA step.
gene	A part of DNA that (via RNA), in suitable circumstances, produces a protein.
genotype	The hereditary character (genes) of an individual.
phenotype	The perceptible properties of an individual.
mutation	A change in the DNA of an organism.
penetrance	The extent to which a gene manifests itself in a certain population.
expressivity	The strength with which a gene manifests itself in an individual.
dominant	The property of a hereditary condition caused by a gene, the inheritance of which from one of the parents is enough for this condition to develop.
recessive	The property of a hereditary condition that will develop only if the gene causing it is inherited from both parents.
chromosome	A part of DNA (much longer than a gene). The human cell contains 46 chromosomes, organised in pairs, 23 from each parent.
sex chromosomes	The pair of chromosomes that decides the sex of the organism. In humans a female has two X chromosomes, a male has one X and one Y chromosome.
modifying gene	A gene that affects the penetrance and/or expressivity of another gene.

Huntington's disease is a dominant single gene disorder that causes severe and progressive physical and neurological deterioration. The symptoms usually become apparent when the affected person is thirty-five to forty-five years old. Symptoms are lack of coordination, lack of balance and an unsteady walking gait, drastic changes in behaviour such as irrational outbursts of rage and increasing physical and mental dysfunction. The disease is not lethal in itself but the symptoms cause other problems, and the person usually dies from these side effects within fifteen to twenty years. The sick individual will be in increasing need of care and will in the end be totally dependent on constant help. Although the genetic cause of the disease is known, no treatment exists for it. Medical treatment aimed at slowing down the process of deterioration is being developed.

Experts believe that about 5–10 per cent of all cancer is caused by hereditary factors. Some are believed to be dominant single gene disorders, with reduced penetrance. One example is the mutation called BRCA1, which can cause breast or ovarian cancer. A carrier of BRCA1 has an approximately 80 per cent risk of developing cancer in adulthood. What you really inherit is then not cancer, but a severely increased risk that you will develop some forms of cancer. As opposed to Huntington's there are, however, methods of treating cancer. There are also preventive measures, such as regular checks and prophylactic surgery (i.e. removal of tissue or complete body parts before symptoms develop).

There are many single gene disorders (about 8,000 have been detected), although all of them are rare. Only a minority of these diseases have their onset in adult years. Presymptomatic genetic testing can today be used to detect some of these diseases and, in principle, such tests can be developed for all of them.

Other diseases are *polygenetic*, that is, they are the result of multiple genes with different loci, each with a small but cumulative effect. There are probably no polygenetic disorders that result solely from the genes involved. Most probably they are all the product of several genes in interaction with environmental factors. These diseases are called *multifactorial*. From this point on, therefore, both polygenetic and multifactorial diseases will be called multifactorial. The term polygenetic will instead be used to refer to the genetic element that is causally active in a multifactorial genetic disease. The inheritance of multifactorial diseases is more complex, and therefore more difficult to predict, than single gene disorders. Predictive testing for multifactorial diseases can therefore only, at best, reveal the risk of disease.

The line between single gene and multifactorial inheritance is not very clear, however. This is because of the existence of genes that influence the penetrance and expressivity of single gene disorders: *modifying genes*. In these cases there is a 'main gene' that causes the symptoms, but it is the modifying gene that affects the onset of the symptoms, the severity of the symptoms and so on. Not all damage to a gene that usually causes disease actually results in disease, since modifying genes also influence the penetrance of the damaged gene. Thus, the damaged gene gives rise only to an increased probability of becoming ill (one example is the cancer case mentioned above).

The fact that single gene disorders may have reduced penetrance makes the common distinction between presymptomatic and predictive genetic testing questionable. It is easy to get the impression that a positive result of a presymptomatic genetic test shows without doubt that the tested individual will become ill (at least if he lives long enough). This, as we have explained, is not the case. The following statement also speaks against the distinction: all predictive genetic testing is presymptomatic (is done

Table 2.2. *Types of genetic diseases and tests, and explanations*

Genetic diseases and tests	Explanation
presymptomatic genetic testing	Genetic testing before the onset of disease to establish the existence of single gene disorders which are very likely to cause disease. Sometimes used as a term for both presymptomatic and predictive genetic testing.
predictive genetic testing	Genetic testing before the onset of disease to establish the risk of developing a polygenetic or multifactorial disease.
genetic carrier detection	Genetic testing to establish whether the individual is a healthy carrier of (recessive) genes that may cause disease in offspring.
single gene disorder	Disease due to damage to a single gene.
polygenetic disease	The genetic basis of diseases due to damage to several genes in combination with environmental factors.
multifactorial disease	Disease due to several genes at different loci in the DNA molecule that interact with environmental factors. Here used for both polygenetic and multifactorial diseases.

before symptoms emerge) and (almost) all presymptomatic testing is predictive (reveals different degrees of risks).

Most diseases of interest to insurance companies are multifactorial: cardiac diseases, alcoholism, diabetes, Alzheimer's disease, schizophrenia and many other diseases can, but do not have to, be the result of a complicated interaction between environmental factors and genes. They might also be the result of environmental factors only. In other words, genes cannot be the sole cause of these diseases, and may not be involved at all. Genetic testing is therefore an imprecise tool for determining the risk of such diseases.

In this context it should also be mentioned that specific combinations of genes can have positive effects on health, even if in other combinations they cause disease. Some individuals thus have inherited 'disease genes' that reduce the risk of contracting infectious diseases such as malaria, tuberculosis and dysentery (Diamond, 1999, p. 201).

Already at this point we can see problems with the classic dichotomy between inheritance and environment. The gene is active in a chemical environment, which influences the gene and can be influenced by external factors. The gene itself can therefore be seen as an easily influenced environmental factor among others. This makes the prospect bleak for many forms of crude genetic essentialism, according to which we are nothing but our genes, and genetic determinism, according to which we are the products of our genes alone. The environment always plays a crucial role in the health and development of the individual.

2.3   The possibilities of genetics

Thus far, this account of genetics has dealt with its past and present achievements. In this section we shall discuss the future potential of this science with regard to the prediction of disease and premature death.

The rapid development of genetics has encouraged the opinion that the genetic basis of a growing number of diseases will be revealed. The received wisdom seems to be that increasing genetic insights will also increase the possibility of predicting disease and length of life. This opinion seems to have been the very fuel that has kept the debate on insurance companies' access to genetic information going. However, scepticism in this regard has been growing recently.[8] The mapping of the human genome – the HUGO project – has recently been concluded and has revealed that human beings have far fewer genes than previously thought (about 30,000 rather than 100,000).[9] The resulting conclusion seems to be not that things are simpler than we had expected, but rather the opposite; the connection between health and genes is more complicated than previously imagined. This is because fewer traits of the phenotype than had been assumed are the result of a single gene. Instead, they are the product of a complex interaction between different genetic[10] and (other) environmental factors, that is multifactorial (Wahlström, 2002). If this analysis, based on the HUGO project, turns out to be correct, there may not be many meaningful predictions we can make about a person's susceptibility to diseases on the basis of genetic testing alone (Göring et al., 2001).[11]

---

[8] See for instance Kristoffersson, 2000, who questions the ability of genetics to make adequate predictions of risk for multifactorial diseases.

[9] This has been questioned too. Geneticists at the Johns Hopkins University now seem to believe (private communication) that the number of genes is somewhere in between (about 70,000), making the scepticism expressed here slightly less valid.

[10] The complexity here results from, among other things, the fact that many genes can be involved in the explanation of a certain trait, that a few genes are sufficient for a wide variety of possible combinations of inheritance (three are enough to yield 64 possibilities), and that some genes affect the penetrance of other genes to various degrees.

[11] Göring et al. are genetic statisticians. They emphasise the difficulty of determining the contribution of a single gene to a trait by statistical methods. In other words: we cannot account for differences in phenotype in terms of differences in genes when a certain trait of the phenotype is multifactorial. This is because the penetration of the DNA loci investigated will always be overvalued with regard to the trait investigated (they can even be completely independent).

The difficulty of making adequate predictions of multifactorial disease on the basis of genetic testing alone is thus explained by the fact that a number of genes, together with various environmental factors and an element of chance, interact to change the cell protein and cause disease. Because all of these factors interact to cause a disease it is difficult to determine the contribution of any one factor in isolation and thus to make predictions on the basis of genetic information alone.

This conclusion is well illustrated by a common form of diabetes, which is multifactorial. Today twelve different genes are considered to affect whether a person will develop the disease or not. This implies *at least* 531,144 possible combinations of alleles.[12] Since different genes have different penetrance and expressivity, and since the environment also influences the risk of diabetes, it is easy to understand why genetic testing will have marginal value as a predictive instrument in this case.

Geneticists, to be sure, think that more single gene disorders will be identified. Presymptomatic genetic testing will probably be developed for these diseases. However, they are rare and there is reason to believe that those not yet discovered are even more rare than those already discovered (otherwise they would probably have been discovered before). The most common and most widespread diseases with an inherited component are multifactorial. They also continue to be explained more by differences in environment than by differences in genes (Kristofferson, 2000, p. 5499).

The future potential of genetic risk analysis must therefore be judged with caution. Visions of how genetics can alter our lives and society to its very foundations may never be realised (Silver, 1997). Today there is not much support for the opinion that genetic testing can be used adequately to determine the risk of most multifactorial diseases.

Even if there are reasons for caution, it is nevertheless important to note that the science of genetics is still relatively young. It is a known fact regarding the history of science that many developments generally considered to be incredible, or even inconceivable, in the scientific community have been realised. Our ability to foresee scientific progress is weak even in the short term, since a certain development is often considered credible only when it is almost a fact. In the mid-1930s, the father of atomic theory, Ernest Rutherford, expressed his conviction that the theory would never have practical applications. About a decade later, the

---

[12] The reservation 'at least' is made due to the Mendelian conjecture that there are two alleles in each gene (one from the mother and one from the father), which can be similar in two ways (AA or aa) or can differ in one way (Aa = aA). There are also reasons to believe that there may be more alleles in a gene, which makes this a cautious estimation of possible combinations.

first atomic bomb exploded (Glover, 1984, p. 14). The common opinion among geneticists was that cloning was not possible, at least not in the foreseeable future, until someone in fact achieved it (remember Dolly, the famous sheep).

However, this account of genetics will not rest on hypotheses concerning developments that are possible, but highly unlikely. The question is to what extent useful and adequate presymptomatic and predictive genetic testing will be developed. There is unanimity on the opinion that tests will be developed for more diseases, but no one knows for which diseases nor how common they are. As we have said, a common view is that they will be developed for more single gene disorders, but not for most of the multifactorial diseases.

Further considerations, however, seem to lend some support to the opinion that reliable predictive genetic testing will be developed for multi-factorial diseases to a larger extent than the sceptics seem to believe. First, not even the sceptics deny that there will be a clearer understanding of the connection between genes and the common diseases (Kristofferson, 2000, p. 5501). This conjecture is strengthened by the suspicion among some geneticists that the HUGO project's way of counting genes may have led to an underestimation of the number of genes (see above). Because of this, it is more likely that a larger number of multifactorial diseases have a simpler pattern of inheritance than the diabetes case mentioned above. As a result, the prospect for reliable and adequate predictive testing seems less bleak. Second, the construction of the biochip or DNA chip has helped to raise expectations of better insights into how genes interact to affect the human organism (Helgesson, 2001).[13] Third, the environment in developed countries has been improved and homogenised, leading to reduced risks of environmentally caused diseases. This may mean that genes will take on increasing significance as a medical risk factor (Rasmusson, 2001). However, one should not disregard the remaining factor, the variation in the inner biological environment of each individual.

Besides tests on DNA (genes), there are other tests that are the result of progress in genetics and that might be used to predict disease or the risk of disease before onset, namely tests on RNA or the protein product. As mentioned in the previous section, the basic doctrine of genetics is that the gene (located on the DNA molecule) creates the protein via RNA. An analysis of the protein product is often used in order to establish a

---

[13] These positive expectations may rest on an underestimation of the complexity of inheritance. In support of this there is the claim that the genes for only a few polygenetic diseases have been identified, in spite of the massive use of biochips.

diagnosis, even for single gene disorders.[14] Two international medical projects, 'functional genomics' and 'proteomics', are studying the relations between damage to RNA or proteins, on the one hand, and diseases, on the other hand. These projects may make it possible to do tests on RNA or proteins that can be used for presymptomatic and predictive purposes, even if the damage to the RNA or the protein has a multifactorial genetic background. To what extent this possibility will be realised is hard to foresee. The tests may not be useful until the individual already has the symptoms of the disease tested for, that is, the change in the RNA or the protein and symptoms may emerge at the same time. In that case, the tests will then become a biochemical test among others used in order to establish or confirm a diagnosis. There will probably be variations: geneticists will be able to reveal (the risk of) some diseases before onset, but not others.

Tests on RNA or protein are not genetic in the strict sense of the word (tests on DNA). In cases where they can be used for presymptomatic and predictive purposes, however, they will not differ in any relevant way from strict genetic testing. The one-sided focus on *genes* in the literature and legislation should therefore cease. Instead, a more inclusive definition of what it is that perhaps should be protected by regulation is appropriate, including biochemical tests on genes and the products of genes in a wider sense.

In this context it is important to mention that insurance companies, for instance, can obtain access to genetic information using other methods besides genetic testing. To an investigator with a proper understanding of genetics, the family's or relatives' medical history can reveal whether a person has a risk of genetically based disease. An insurance company can therefore use family information, rather than genetic testing, in order to acquire relevant genetic information, if regulation is confined to genetic testing as such. If society wishes to prevent discrimination due to genetic information or to protect genetic privacy, it should not focus exclusively on genetic *testing*. Genetic information is, in itself, neutral with regard to method, even if regulation is not.

In view of all these uncertainties regarding the future of genetics, we should experiment with different scenarios. For simplicity, we will use two different kinds of scenario for the next ten to fifteen years. One scenario is more cautious and in line with the opinions of many geneticists today (Göring *et al.*, 2001; Kristoffersson, 2000; Wahlström, 2002). The *cautious scenario* conjectures that we will identify more single gene disorders

---

[14] For instance, phenylketonuria (PKU) is tested this way. PKU is a recessive single gene disorder, which leads to death a few years after birth if the child is not fed a certain diet.

(each one rare), for which reliable presymptomatic genetic testing will probably be developed, but we will not be able to develop reliable predictive testing for most multifactorial diseases. In rare cases, tests on RNA and protein will be possible before the onset of the disease, but will mainly be used to establish a diagnosis, since in most cases damage to the RNA or protein and the disease will emerge at the same time.

The *bold scenario* agrees with the cautious scenario that more single gene disorders will be detectable before onset through presymptomatic genetic testing. However, the bold scenario has more faith in the possibility of developing reliable predictive genetic testing for multifactorial diseases. It also has higher hopes concerning the possibility of using RNA or protein tests for presymptomatic and predictive purposes. The most plausible version of the bold scenario emphasises the latter rather than the former possibility.

For the purpose of the ensuing deliberations, the practical difference between the scenarios is that in the cautious one only a small proportion of the population can be demonstrated to suffer from genetic defects, while in the bold one, genetic testing can reveal differences in insurance risks for much wider population groups.

Will the cautious or the bold scenario be realised? The cautious scenario perhaps has a stronger foundation, given the opinions of geneticists today. We have deliberately cast the bold scenario in vague terms, in order to allow different degrees of deviation from the cautious scenario. It is legitimate to ask why we should experiment with scenarios that appear less likely to occur given the well-founded beliefs of today's geneticists. We have already hinted at the answer to that question: scientific development is hard to predict, even in the short term. Scientific achievement often surpasses the most fanciful prognoses for the future. Even if the bold scenario at present seems less likely, we should consider the societal consequences of that scenario too, so that we shall not be taken by surprise if it should be realised after all. The realisation of some version of the bold scenario will be a severe test for politicians and shapers of public opinion, and bearing in mind the inertia of political institutions there is good reason to formulate a strategy now that enables us to handle the consequences of that scenario, should it come about.

One or two further possibilities of genetics are worth mentioning in this context. Many genetic diseases cannot be treated today (e.g. Huntington's disease). However, one of the primary motives behind the HUGO project was to develop effective therapies for such diseases, or at least medicines that delay or lessen the severity of the symptoms. There are reasons for optimism about the chances of success in this endeavour. Presymptomatic and predictive testing – on DNA, RNA or protein – will then be useful in order to offer treatment before the onset of the disease. On the other hand, such treatment costs money, for which insurance, whether public or private, is necessary. Already preventive measures can be offered for some presymptomatically diagnosed genetic diseases, such as recommendations of changes in lifestyle or prophylactic treatment.

Only two years ago, when we were preparing the Swedish edition of our book, we predicted that genetic 'home tests' would be available on the market in ten to fifteen years' time. These tests would enable individuals to find out about their genetic propensity to various conditions, without ever coming into contact with public health care. This prediction has already been fulfilled, demonstrating the pace at which developments are progressing. In the United States genetic home tests that reveal the risk of developing a certain form of breast cancer (section 2.2) can be ordered by mail, and in London, genetic tests that reveal sensitivity to certain diets can be bought directly in shops.[15] The results of such tests may well be absent from an individual's medical records, with the possible consequence that while more and more people will have access to genetic information with great relevance to estimating health and life expectancy, this information will be kept private.[16]

2.4   Consequences for private personal insurance

As we have seen, genetics is in its infancy. However, it has already created a lively, sometimes aggressive debate about the potential ethical, economic and social consequences of letting insurance companies use genetic information when assessing risks relating to health, life and pension insurance. As a result of the debate, many countries have implemented regulations

---

[15] In the United States the tests are provided by Myriard Genetics in Salt Lake City (Capron, 2000) and in the United Kingdom by Sconia (www.genewatch.org).

[16] The home test scenario raises several questions which we will not address fully here, while briefly mentioning a few. For instance, it is questionable whether it is desirable that individuals are allowed to test themselves outside the scope of the public health care system, which provides genetic counsellors to help the individual to understand the complicated probabilities that the results of genetic testing may reveal. Without such counselling, the individual might misinterpret the results of the test and either under- or overestimate their significance (which may lead to the absence of much needed treatment or prevention on the one hand or needless worry on the other). Another possible consequence of the home test scenario is that the results of genetic testing can more easily be withheld from insurance companies than when this information is part of the tested individual's medical records. This will make it difficult effectively to uphold a regulation that forbids individuals to withhold genetic information if available (partial regulation).

that forbid insurance companies to demand genetic investigations as a precondition for insurance (partial regulation), and which furthermore often prevent the companies from asking for information from previous tests (total regulation). The question of regulation will be of immediate interest in more countries, as genetic testing (and other biochemical testing procedures resulting from developments in genetics) will become more common in diagnosing and predicting disease.

Genetic tests currently offer the possibility of assessing the risk of a limited number of relatively unusual diseases. Only a small portion of the total population has taken such tests and among the population in general there are very few who have reason to consider testing. Because of this, restricting insurance companies' access to genetic information does not pose any serious threat to their viability today.

The determination and differentiation of premiums on the basis of actuarial assessments of risk can be expected to differ depending on whether insurance companies are allowed or forbidden to use genetic information. The insurance industry runs the risk of collapse due to increasing problems with asymmetric information and adverse selection if it is not granted access to the results of genetic testing while many of its customers have such information. These customers, acting on the basis of genetic risk assessments, can then buy insurance providing very high benefits while keeping the risk information to themselves – information that would have led to higher premiums due to the increased risk if revealed to the company. The problem will become particularly severe if some insurance companies are able to avoid regulation by moving their operations abroad.

The seriousness of the problem of adverse selection depends to some extent on whether the cautious or the bold scenario turns out to be nearer the truth. If the bold scenario is realised, in ten to fifteen years' time genetics will be able to offer drastically refined methods of determining the risk of disease and premature death for a wide range of diseases and for large population groups. This would enable a great number of individuals to profit from this knowledge by buying insurance at premiums that do not reflect the risk they represent. However, the bold scenario seems currently more unlikely than the cautious.

Yet even the cautious scenario will result in increased problems with adverse selection during the next ten to fifteen years, partly because it will be possible to use other biochemical tests, also a result of the progress in genetics, for presymptomatic and predictive purposes. Furthermore, the increased use of genetic testing in clinical settings will result in more people knowing about their genetic susceptibility to disease. This in itself will give more people the opportunity to use that information to buy insurance without revealing the level of risk.

The seriousness of the problem of adverse selection will also vary to some extent with the form of insurance. The problem is absent in the case of pension insurance, since high-risk individuals will lower their pension premiums (they are less likely to reach pensionable age).[17] The problem is perhaps most evident in the case of premature death insurance, where the amount of compensation is determined almost exclusively by the insurer and the insured person together, and the latter has an obvious interest in keeping information about heightened risk of premature death to himself. Adverse selection is probably somewhat less of a problem in the case of health insurance, since compensation for treatment is partly determined by its cost. However, when it comes to compensation for income, benefits and thus also premiums can vary to a larger degree.

Of course, the development of genetics will also provide means of reducing the risk of disease and premature death. For some multifactorial diseases, the probability of getting ill can be reduced by changes in lifestyle. But even so, the risk will probably still be greater than average, which provides an incentive for keeping the information from the insurance companies. And even if the risk can be eliminated through medical therapy or other prophylactic measures (which will probably happen in some cases, see 2.3), treatment costs money. Insurance companies will therefore raise the premiums for these people, who again will have an incentive to acquire personal insurance without revealing the eliminable risk.

It is also important to keep in mind that even if the relations between genes and diseases are so complicated as to defy any simplistic account of their connection, this does not bother insurance companies. Given absence of regulation, insurance companies may increasingly use genetic markers to differentiate high-risk populations, even if it is not the gene (or genes) in itself (themselves) that causes the increased risk. Insurance companies are interested in statistical rather than causal relations.

This is illustrated by the use of gender as a differentiating factor for pension insurance. Even if it is true that not all women live longer than all men and that being a woman does not on its own give rise to a longer life, it is true that women on average live longer than men. This alone is enough to give women higher premiums for pensions. If insurance companies are denied the right to use genetic information, they are denied a tool for differentiating high-risk populations. This tool can instead be used to their detriment.

---

[17] However, the problem resurfaces if genetic tests can demonstrate a high probability of a very long life, for such individuals will have a strong incentive to invest heavily in pension schemes.

Given all this it becomes more important for politicians to ponder whether regulations to limit insurance companies' access to genetic information will achieve the intended goals. They should also consider whether these goals are of greater value than the drawbacks that regulation entails for insurance companies and, as a consequence, for society at large. These problems are the main theme of the chapters that follow.

3 Opportunities for insurers to use genetic information

3.1 Background: duty of disclosure and balance of information

In the draft proposal for the current Swedish Insurance Contracts Act[1] the section concerning the policy-holder's duty of disclosure begins as follows.

When an insurance contract is concluded it is important that the insurer receives precise information about the circumstances that are of relevance to an actuarial assessment of the nature and scope of risks for which the insurance policy intends to provide protection. This information is necessary first and foremost in order to decide whether or not insurance protection can be provided at all. Without detailed information about specific circumstances it is, as a rule, impossible to calculate the fee that will have to be paid in the form of the premium to the insurer, or to determine the terms that shall apply to the insurance policy in general. The most obvious course in this respect is to adhere to the information provided by the applicant, who must be generally assumed to be able to gather information easily about the existing factual circumstances. (SOU 1925:21, p. 68, authors' translation)

The quotation expresses an internationally widely accepted view that in connection with any application for insurance the insurer has to decide, taking into consideration the risk in question, whether that risk is insurable at all, and if so, the premium that will be required for the desired insurance cover.[2] It further transpires that the responsibility for providing the insurer with necessary information ought to rest with the policy-holder, as the one who usually possesses or at least can easily get hold of the information in question. These principles are expressed in the legislation by the provisions concerning the duty of disclosure. Under these provisions the policy-holder is responsible for providing the insurer with correct information concerning circumstances that may be assumed to be of importance for the latter. If the policy-holder fails to satisfy his duty of

---

[1] Försäkringsavtalslag (1927:77).

[2] As is well known, the reason for this is that insurance companies have to be able to discharge their obligations towards the policy-holders in any situation.

disclosure, the right to compensation in case of damage will cease to exist either wholly or partly. This sanction is not applicable, however, if the inadequate information can be regarded as due to an excusable mistake on the part of the policy-holder, who was either unaware or could not be expected to be aware of a certain circumstance or its importance for the insurer.[3]

The legislator's point of departure is thus the view that at the time of concluding the contract the insurer shall have the same information regarding the risk as the policy-holder. One can speak here of a fundamental requirement for a balance of information between the parties which is to be ensured by means of the provisions concerning the policy-holder's duty of disclosure.

From the mid-1990s on, however, a growing number of countries have introduced regulations that in varying degrees exempt genetic information from the duty of disclosure. This chapter describes these regulations (section 3.2), as well as their problematic consequences (section 3.3) and the reasons why the regulations are felt to be justified despite these consequences (3.4). Section 3.5 contains some concluding remarks.

3.2   The regulations

Restrictions concerning the insurer's access to genetic information are expressed in various different forms. At international level a convention and various different recommendations and declarations can be found (section 3.2.1). At national level there is legislation (section 3.2.2) as well as a number of voluntary agreements (section 3.2.3). Section 3.2.4 examines the relationship between the existing regulations and the two concepts of partial and total regulation that are used in this account. Finally, section 3.2.5 discusses the possible shape, direction and formulation of future regulations.

3.2.1   International conventions, recommendations and declarations

The insurer's right to use the results of genetic testing is regulated by the Convention on Human Rights and Biomedicine adopted by the Council of Europe in 1996,[4] Article 12 of which stipulates that presymptomatic and predictive genetic testing may be performed for health care purposes

---

[3] This constitutes a greatly simplified summary of the legal rules concerning the insured party's duty of disclosure in most of western Europe.

[4] ETS no. 164. The Convention, which came into force in 1999, had been ratified by the autumn of 2002 by only a small number of countries.

or for health-related scientific research only. Genetic testing for other purposes (for example in connection with insurance) is thus prohibited.

Article 11 of the Convention, moreover, contains a prohibition against any form of discrimination on the basis of an individual's genetic heritage. Even though is not spelt out explicitly, the prohibition concerns only unfair discrimination (Explanatory Report, 1996, Article 11). This being so, representatives of the insurance industry claim that discrimination based on actuarial grounds is not to be regarded as unfair discrimination and that the provisions therefore do not affect insurance underwriting practices (Lemmens, 2000, pp. 358 f.). However, no real support for the view that actuarial discrimination ought to be considered fair has been propounded.

The qualifier 'unfair' seems rather to be intended to make it clear that the concept of discrimination does not include affirmative action benefiting those already suffering unfair treatment because of genetic conditions (Explanatory Report, 1996, Article 11 and Lemmens, 2000, p. 359). Thus there is much to support the view that Article 11 of the Convention, among other things, prohibits insurers from using the results of genetic testing when considering applications for personal insurance policies. To all appearances insurance companies will not even be allowed to discriminate on the basis of so-called family history, since such discrimination must be regarded as based on the individual's genetic heritage. Such a situation would be, however, in stark contrast to what is usual in insurance underwriting practices in a large number of countries (cf. Lemmens, 2000, p. 359). It is therefore likely that many countries will take the opportunity to make reservations against provisions conflicting with their national legislation in connection with ratification of the Convention (Article 36 and Lemmens, 2000, p. 359).

Under Article 23 the parties to the Convention shall be responsible for the provision of appropriate judicial procedures to prevent unlawful infringement of the rights and principles set forth in the Convention. This clause refers to both anticipated and ongoing infringements of the provisions and is regarded as requiring an ability to intervene at short notice (Explanatory Report, 1996, Article 23). Further, under Article 25 the parties shall provide for appropriate sanctions in the event of infringement of the provisions of the Convention. Article 24 lays down the principle that a person who has suffered damage as a result of illegitimate restrictions of the rights enshrined in the Convention is entitled to compensation in accordance with the rules applying in the signatory country in question.

In addition to the Convention a number of recommendations and declarations concerning genetic discrimination can be found at international level. One of these recommendations was adopted by the Council of Europe as early as 1992.[5] It proclaims that the insurer has no right to require that genetic testing be performed, nor to enquire about results of earlier genetic tests in connection with an insurance policy application. Another declaration, adopted by UNESCO in 1997,[6] specifies that no one shall be subjected to discrimination on the basis of genetic character- istics which is intended to violate, or does actually violate, human rights, fundamental freedoms or human dignity.[7] Even though recommenda- tions and declarations of this kind[8] are not binding, they may be consid- ered to express internationally recognised political tendencies, indicating a possible course for future national and international legislation.

3.2.2   Legislation

In a number of countries opportunities for insurance companies to use the results of genetic testing have been restricted by means of legislation. In order to illustrate these restrictions this section discusses legislation introduced in Norway and Denmark in the 1990s, concerning insur- ance companies' access to genetic information. Our decision to discuss the legislation of these two countries is due primarily to the fact that it constitutes a good example of how strict the regulation of the issues con- cerned can be. At the same time the short account of the legislation in some other continental European countries and the United States, which is presented at the end of this section, demonstrates that the legislation in Norway and Denmark is in no way unique.[9]

In Norway the Act on Medical Use of Biotechnology was adopted as early as in 1994.[10] Chapter 6 of the Act discusses genetic testing after birth.[11] Under Section 6-2, genetic testing may be used in medical con- texts only for the purposes of diagnosis and/or treatment. Presymptomatic and predictive tests as well as diagnosis of genetic susceptibility require,

---

[5] Recommendation No. R (92) 3 on Genetic Testing and Screening for Health Care Purposes.

[6] Universal Declaration on the Human Genome and Human Rights of 11 November 1997.

[7] Ibid., Article 6.

[8] The reader may also wish to refer to similar documents issued by the World Medical Association and the World Health Organisation.

[9] At this stage the reader's attention may be drawn to the fact that genetic testing for diagnostic purposes is most often treated more liberally than other types of genetic testing. This is further elaborated in the following paragraphs and in table 3.1.

[10] Lov av 5 August 1994 nr 56 om medisinsk bruk av bioteknologi.

[11] In accordance with S. 6-1 of the Act, genetic testing refers to the different types of tests listed in chapter 2 of this book. In addition, the concept of 'genetic testing' covers genetic laboratory testing for the determination of gender, with the exception of tests performed for the purpose of identification.

additionally, the tested person's consent (Section 6-4) and authorisation from the relevant ministry (the Ministry of Health and Social Welfare – Section 6-3).

It is further prohibited under Section 6-7, subsection 1, to request, receive, possess or use information about another person which has come to light in conjunction with genetic testing for other than diagnostic purposes. Subsection 2 goes so far as to prohibit asking whether genetic tests have been performed. Subsections 3 to 5 contain, however, a number of exceptions from these provisions. These include, among other things, information about existing diseases discovered in connection with genetic testing for the purposes of diagnosis.[12] Both insurers and other parties[13] are otherwise effectively hindered from using information about individuals' DNA. Violations of the prohibitions contained in the Act are punishable by fine or prison for up to three months (Section 8-5).

The regulatory framework in Denmark does not have this general character. But the question of a third-party right to use health information has attracted attention in at least two specific contexts. Since 1996 there has been a law prohibiting the unwarranted use of information about a person's health status to limit an employee's opportunity to obtain work or keep his or her job.[14] In the field of insurance too, the possibilities of using medical information about a person's health have become the object of regulation. In 1997 a provision was introduced in Section 3a of the Danish insurance contract law,[15] prohibiting insurance companies from requesting, obtaining, or receiving and using, in connection with the conclusion of an insurance contract, information that can shed light on a person's genetic predisposition and the genetic risk of developing or contracting a disease. The prohibition does not apply, however, to information – genetic or other – concerning the insured person's or other persons' present or earlier state of health. Violations are punishable by fine as laid down in Section 134.[16]

To summarise, it can be said that Norwegian and Danish laws in the area have similar effects. The results of presymptomatic and predictive testing and diagnosis of genetic predispositions may not be used in insurance underwriting at all. Insurers may not request that such tests be conducted as prerequisites for insurance cover or demand results of earlier tests of this kind. On the other hand, both Danish and Norwegian

---

[12] None of the other exceptions are relevant in the present context.
[13] For example employers and banks.
[14] Lov no. 286 of 24 April 1996 om brug af helbredsoplysninger mv på arbejdsmarkedet.
[15] Lovbekendtgørelse 1986-10-24 nr. 726 om forsikkringsaftaler.
[16] Equivalent provisions have been introduced into the Act on the supervision of corporate pension funds (Ss. 9a and 71) (Bekendtørelse nr. 777 of 17/08/2000 af lov om tilsn med firmapensionskasser).

insurance companies may demand and take account of the results of earlier genetic tests performed for diagnostic purposes. Under Danish law insurance companies are even considered free to require that an insurance applicant shall undergo such testing as a condition for obtaining insurance. Under Norwegian law genetic testing may only be performed for medical purposes. As regards family history no express restrictions can be found in either Norwegian or Danish law.[17] Insurance companies in both countries may also escape liability for hereditary diseases by various exemption clauses, thus avoiding any problems that may arise in connection with the regulatory framework under discussion.[18]

In continental Europe, Belgium and Austria have adopted legislation similar to that described above. In these countries insurers can neither require genetic testing of applicants nor use genetic test results that are already available in medical records (Lemmens, 2000, p. 360; Fotheringham, 1999, p. 21; Rosén, 1999, p. 167). Statutes of this kind can also be found in France and the Netherlands, although they do not have such radical effects as in the above-mentioned countries. In France it is forbidden to conduct genetic testing for other than medical purposes or for scientific research. This does not prevent insurers from obtaining genetic test information from medical files in order to use them for risk assessment (Lemmens, 2000, p. 361; Rosén, 1999, p. 167).[19] In the Netherlands a statute on medical examinations prevents insurers from requiring applicants to submit to medical examinations, including genetic tests, which may indicate the presence of a serious and incurable disease (Rosén, 1999, p. 167).[20]

In the United States the use of both genetic test results and family history for group insurance purposes is prohibited by federal legislation (O'Neill, 1998, p. 719). Other than that no legislation exists in the area at federal level. A number of states, among others New Jersey, have adopted legislation extending the above-mentioned prohibition to individual health insurance (Lemmens, 2000, p. 362; O'Neill, 1998, p. 719).

---

[17] There have been discussions, however, on whether the prohibition of S. 6-7(1) of the Norwegian act ought to be considered to include information obtained by means of family history (see NOU 2000:23, pp. 69 f.). The arguments propounded in support of this extensive interpretation cannot be regarded as wholly convincing, however.

[18] See table 3.1.

[19] The French insurance companies have decided, however, to refrain from taking account of genetic information in connection with the handling of applications for personal insurance (Lemmens, 2000, p. 361). Concerning such voluntary decisions see section 3.2.3.

[20] As in France this legislation has been temporarily supplemented by the insurance sector's undertaking to refrain from using genetic information when handling applications for personal insurance (Lemmens, 2000, p. 360). See section 3.2.3.

Regarding life insurance, restrictions concerning the access of insurance companies to genetic information are rare.

3.2.3 Voluntary agreements

In several countries voluntary and temporary agreements entail restrictions which resemble those following from the Norwegian and Danish statutes. The reason why these countries have chosen to refrain from legislation seems to be the prevailing uncertainty regarding the actuarial implications of genetic technology (Fotheringham, 1999, p. 20; Rosén, 1999, p. 168), and also the view that the current issue has not been studied thoroughly enough (cf. Skr 1998/99:136, p. 33).

In order to illustrate what agreements of this kind usually look like, we shall examine the agreement concerning insurance companies' access to genetic information concluded between the Swedish state and the Swedish Insurance Federation. The reason for looking at this particular agreement is that it shows how these types of agreements are typically formulated – a point which is clearly evident from the short account at the end of this section of agreements of this type concluded in a number of other west European countries.

In 1999, an agreement was concluded between the Swedish state and the Swedish Insurance Federation concerning genetic testing in connection with taking out what is referred to in insurance contract law as life and health insurance.[21] The agreement was based on a 1997 covenant between the Federation's members whose objective was to counteract criticism which had been levelled at the possibilities of genetic discrimination by insurance companies (Flood, 1999, p. 18; Mattsson, 2001, p. 311). According to Section 2 of the agreement, the concept of genetic testing focuses on presymptomatic and predictive testing as well as genetic susceptibility diagnostics. Genetic testing performed for the purpose of diagnosing diseases therefore falls outside the scope of the agreement. Swedish insurers may therefore freely demand that such testing be performed as well as request and use the results.

The most important parts of the agreement can be found in Sections 3–4. Under Section 3, insurance companies are not allowed to demand that an insurance applicant shall undergo a genetic test as a prerequisite for granting or augmenting an insurance policy. Under Section 4, insurance companies may not demand to know whether genetic testing has

---

[21] So-called children's insurance, which consists of combined accident and health insurance, is not covered by the agreement. Occupational group life insurance or occupational sickness insurance, in which health information is not required, are also not covered by the agreement (S. 1).

been performed, nor enquire about the results of such tests or the family medical history. In cases when an insurer already knows the results of an existing genetic test or has access to family history, the Insurance Federation undertakes to ensure that this information shall not be taken into account. This rule does not apply, however, if (i) the insurance policy amount to be paid out as a lump sum in the case of illness or death exceeds the equivalent of some US$61,000; or (ii) if the insurance amount to be paid upon the insured party's illness or death in the form of periodically paid compensation, survivor's pension, or survivor's annuity exceeds some US$4,000 a year (Section 4(2)).[22] As is the case with Section 3, this provision applies to applications both for new insurance and to augment existing insurance policies (Section 4(4)).

Under Section 5, moreover, insurance companies are not allowed to exclude any diseases from the scope of the insurance policies affected by the agreement. This does not apply, however, to a condition whose symptoms were already visible at the time of the conclusion of the insurance policy.

Finally, under Section 6 of the agreement, the Insurance Federation undertakes to set up a board of inquiry to which insurance applicants who are dissatisfied with the insurer's handling of genetic information may turn.

The agreement was concluded on 1 July 1999 and is valid until 2002 with a possibility of extension (Section 8).

A comparison shows that like their Danish and Norwegian colleagues, Swedish insurers are not allowed to require that the applicant shall undergo genetic tests of a presymptomatic or predictive nature or diagnostic tests to determine genetic susceptibility in connection with the issuing of new policies or augmenting life and health insurance. Nothing prevents Swedish insurers, though, from requiring that the applicant shall undergo genetic tests for the purpose of diagnosing diseases. In this respect the Swedish regulation corresponds to the Danish legislation, but not the Norwegian, under which no genetic testing whatsoever may be performed for other than medical purposes. Another similarity is that Swedish, Danish and Norwegian insurers may not ask for results from either presymptomatic or predictive genetic tests, or of diagnostic tests concerning genetic susceptibility.

In some respects the Swedish regulatory framework is more far-reaching, however, than the Norwegian and Danish ones. In contrast to their Danish and Norwegian colleagues, Swedish insurers may not even use family history. Furthermore it is provided that no insurer may

---

[22] Over time, both these figures have been adjusted for inflation.

evade the risks that these prohibitions entail by excluding hereditary diseases from the insurance policy. Neither the Danish nor the Norwegian legislation prevents insurers from applying such exclusions.

In one important respect the Swedish prohibitions are far from being as extensive as their Norwegian and Danish counterparts. The Swedish prohibition against requesting and taking account of the results of earlier genetic tests, including family history, applies only up to a specified insurance amount. If the insurance amount is higher than that, Swedish insurance companies may request and take account of the results of both presymptomatic and predictive genetic tests as well as genetic susceptibility diagnostics.

For an overview of the conditions in the three countries see table 3.1.

Agreements similar to the Swedish one can be found, for example, in the Netherlands and the United Kingdom.[23] These agreements have been concluded, like the Swedish agreement, to avoid criticism of either discrimination or legislation following from insurance companies having access to genetic tests (Lemmens, 2000, p. 361). As in Sweden insurance companies in these countries have undertaken to refrain from requiring applicants to undergo genetic testing of a presymptomatic and predictive character or diagnostic tests to determine genetic susceptibility. Results of earlier tests of this type that are available in medical records, moreover, may not be used other than when the insurance amount exceeds certain limit values. These limit values exceed the Swedish limit values by a large margin, however (Flood, 1999, p. 107; Fotheringham, 1999, pp. 19 ff.; Lemmens, 2000, pp. 360 f.; Rosén, 1999, pp. 167 f.; O'Neill, 1998, pp. 720 ff.).[24]

3.2.4   Partial and total regulation

It has been shown that the regulatory situation applying to insurance companies' access to genetic information is rather complex. This is primarily due to the fact that the tenor of the regulations varies depending on the purpose of the genetic test (table 3.1). The complexity is compounded by

---

[23] As can be seen in section 3.2.2 the French insurance companies have also voluntarily entered into commitments similar to those described in the following (Lemmens, 2000, p. 361).

[24] British insurance companies are allowed in insurance policies exceeding the limit values to use only such information as is regarded as admissible by the government's Genetics and Insurance Committee (GAIC). Until January 2002 GAIC had allowed only one type of genetic information to be used, namely information about Huntington's disease, which can be used in connection with selling life insurance (Association of British Insurers, 2002).

Table 3.1. *Scope of regulations in Norway, Denmark and Sweden*

	Norway	Denmark	Sweden
Ability of insurer to require insurance applicant to undergo			
genetic testing for diagnostic purposes	no	yes	yes
presymptomatic genetic testing	no	no	no
predictive genetic testing	no	no	no
diagnostic testing to determine genetic susceptibility	no	no	no
Ability of insurer to use results available in medical records concerning			
genetic tests for diagnostic purposes	yes	yes	yes
presymptomatic genetic tests	no	no	yes, if the amount of insurance exceeds a certain limit value
predictive genetic tests	no	no	yes, if the amount of insurance exceeds a certain limit value
diagnostic tests to determine genetic susceptibility	no	no	yes, if the amount of insurance exceeds a certain limit value
Ability of insurer to use family history	yes	yes	yes, if the amount of insurance exceeds a certain limit value
Ability of insurer exclude hereditary diseases from the scope of the insurance when the contract was concluded	yes	yes	yes, if the applicant showed symptoms

insurance companies' opportunities to make exceptions in certain cases regarding hereditary diseases.

In order to simplify the following presentation we shall focus primarily on the regulations concerning genetic information obtained from presymptomatic and predictive genetic tests and on diagnostic tests to determine genetic susceptibility. To make the understanding of our line of reasoning easier the regulations have been divided (as described in chapter 1) into two main types: partial and total regulation. Partial regulation prohibits insurance companies from requesting that genetic testing be performed as a prerequisite for insurance, but allows them to request results from genetic test information in medical records. Total regulation prohibits the latter as well.

Bearing in mind these simplifications it can be seen that Norway and Denmark already have total regulation and that Swedish regulation is also essentially total. Insofar as the amount of insurance exceeds a certain specified limit value the Swedish regulatory framework changes its guise, becoming partial regulation.

3.2.5   The future

We have shown that many countries located around the north Atlantic have introduced restrictions in the last few years concerning insurance companies' access to genetic information, either by means of statute or agreement.[25] The existing regulations largely amount to what we call total regulation.

Since existing agreements are usually only temporary solutions pending statutory regulation, it is probable that legislation will in future be introduced in many of the countries that now have regulation by agreement only. As stated in chapter 1, such a change will hardly be of any major practical importance.

Since the problems concerning genetic information and insurance are new and their practical importance is increasing, it is likely that regulation in this area will shortly be introduced in a number of countries that do not possess it today. There are strong grounds for supposing that such regulation will be performed by means of legislation and that this will largely take the form of total regulation.

On the other hand it is hardly likely that future regulation will be as categorical as that applied in Norway and Denmark today. It is more probable that regulation will rather resemble the Swedish regulation, which is in principle total, but becomes partial when high insurance amounts are involved. In support of this assumption it can be said that reforms to the Norwegian regulations to this effect have recently been suggested. A bill introduced in 2000 states that Norwegian insurance companies ought to be given the same measure of access to genetic information as to other health information (NOU 2000:23, pp. 69 f.). At the same time it has been suggested that using health-related information should be made unlawful in the case of basic insurance where the amount of insurance is

---

[25] In addition, a number of international conventions, declarations and recommendations exist. The practical importance of these must, however, be regarded as still quite limited.

lower than a stipulated limit value, and in the case of obligatory insurance (NOU 2000:23, p. 61 f.). In the case of insurance amounts above the stipulated value, the applicant may be required to provide information about his health status as well as genetic predisposition. On the other hand, insurance companies are not allowed to request that the insurance applicant shall undergo medical or genetic tests. Such demands are to be allowed, however, if the insurance amount in question exceeds a further stipulated and very high amount (NOU 2000:23, pp. 62 f.). On the whole, the proposal may be considered paradoxical. As regards the question of insurance companies' access to *genetic information*, the proposal entails a certain degree of liberalisation of the regulation now in force. If the proposal is implemented, the regulatory framework will be comparable with that currently applied in Sweden (and also in the Netherlands and the United Kingdom). At the same time it is obvious that insurance companies' access to *other types of health information*, which is currently quite easy, will be sharply restricted. In this respect the proposal must be considered controversial.[26] It remains to be seen whether it will be wholly or only partly implemented.

Finally it can be noted that, surprisingly, no measures have been taken to date by the European Community (EC) in order to prevent genetic discrimination on the part of private insurance companies. In other contexts the EC has acted forcefully to prevent discrimination (see chapter 6, section 6.3.3.2). Also, uniform rules concerning the access of insurance companies to genetic information are of vital importance if the common insurance market created within the Union is to function satisfactorily (see chapter 5, sections 5.3–5.4 regarding the problems that may arise when insurance companies whose access to genetic information becomes limited are forced to compete with companies whose access to such information is unrestricted). In this situation it is probable that uniform restrictions of insurance companies' access to genetic information, similar to those presented in this section, will be established in time in all the member countries.

3.3   Consequences of regulation

3.3.1   Asymmetric information

As has been shown in section 3.1, the legislator has been working on the premise that at the time when the insurance contract is concluded the

---

[26] From another angle, the proposal may be considered more consistent, since there may not be any relevant difference between genetic and other medical information (see section 3.4.3 and chapter 7, section 7.4.2).

Insurer should have the same information about the risk as the insurance applicant. In other words, there should be a balance of information between the parties. If the insurance applicant has never undergone genetic testing he will be as unaware as the insurer about any existing genetic condition. To the extent to which insurance companies are only prevented from requiring, as a condition for providing insurance, that the applicant shall undergo genetic testing (partial regulation), the even balance of information between the parties cannot be considered to be disturbed (Sandberg, 1996, p. 90).

But over and above this, insurance companies are largely prohibited from requesting genetic test results that are available in medical records (total regulation). Since an insurance applicant will normally have access to the results of genetic tests undertaken, it is obvious that in this respect the regulations allow the applicant to have more information at his disposal than the insurance company, so that here we describe the information as asymmetric.

An insurance applicant who knows as a result of an earlier genetic test that he runs the risk of suffering a heart attack at a young age may thus take out personal insurance without informing the insurer of the fact. This applies even in situations when the applicant has realised or should have realised that the information in question is highly relevant for the insurer's risk assessment. The applicant's premium will be equivalent in this case to the premiums charged to persons who do not run increased risks of becoming ill or dying. In cases of insurance against sickness or premature death this means that the applicant's insurance cover will be subsidised by all those who are not at increased risk. In the case of pension insurance without cover for survivors the situation will be reversed. Since the insurance company has not been informed of the fact that the applicant is at risk of early death, he will have to pay a premium that exceeds the expected compensation costs, and in this way subsidise those policy-holders who are expected to live longer than him.

3.3.2   Adverse selection

Subsidies influence demand. If those who are aware that they run a higher-than-average risk of being afflicted by the insured event (the high risks) do not need to inform the insurer about it, they will buy insurance on a particularly large scale. In the same way, persons knowing that they represent a smaller-than-average risk (the low risks) will take out insurance on a particularly limited scale. Loss compensation will therefore exceed income from premiums, as a result of which the premiums will have to be raised. This in turn will cause the demand for insurance on the part of the good risks to decrease further, while the share of bad risks in the insurance collective will become even higher. This will lead to further premium increases. The result is thus a vicious circle with an ever increasing proportion of high risks and constantly rising premiums. In the end, the premiums will become so high that not even the high risks will be interested in obtaining insurance. The insurance market will therefore collapse (Radetzki, 1996, p. 248).[27]

The significance of problems connected with adverse selection (for a discussion, see Lemmens and Bahamin, 1998, pp. 172 ff.) is governed primarily by the degree of asymmetric information. These problems grow with the number of individuals who possess more information about the risk insured against than the insurance company, and with the relevance of this information. The problems associated with adverse selection should therefore also grow as an increasing number of individuals undergo genetic tests, and as these tests provide more sophisticated and reliable information. The significance of adverse selection will thus depend in future on whether genetics follows the bold or the cautious scenario, as described in chapter 2, section 2.3. Beyond this, the scope of the problem of adverse selection is governed to a great extent by the conduct of the low risks. If they can be presumed to show endurance and, because of solidarity, inertia, lack of alternatives or for other reasons, accept a certain measure of subsidisation of the high risks, the effects may be limited. Taking into consideration the ongoing process of globalisation, along with the resulting increasing possibilities of international commerce with insurance services, it is unlikely, however, that the low risks will display so much endurance. If genetics develops according to the bold scenario, it is feasible that in the long run total regulation will entail such a high proportion of adverse selection cases that it will not be able to accomplish its purpose.[28] If, on the other hand, genetics develops according to the more cautious scenario, the significance of adverse selection is more difficult to assess. As has been argued in chapter 2, section 2.3, there are

[27] This is a simplified description of adverse selection and its consequences. For a basic study of both asymmetric information and adverse selection see Akerlof, 1970, pp. 488 ff. Concerning adverse selection the reader may refer to Lemmens and Bahamin, 1998, pp. 171 f.

[28] The fact that the risk of adverse selection is of great practical importance is clearly illustrated by developments regarding the issue of the survivor's cover in the Swedish supplementary pension system. The possibility of obtaining such cover without prior medical examination was supposed to have been introduced in 2002 according to the original plans. In view of the extensive risk of adverse selection its introduction has been postponed, however. See Prop 2001/02:49, pp. 9 f. This case is of particular interest because it is so far one of relatively few examples where legislators have taken adverse selection explicitly into account.

reasons to believe that adverse selection even in this case will entail palpable difficulties for the insurance industry. This view is further developed in chapter 5.

We noted in section 3.2.3 that total regulation in certain countries, among them Sweden, is applied only in so far as the insurance amount is lower than a stipulated limit value. In such an arrangement there is a reduction in the total scope of risks that can be insured on the basis of asymmetric information, and consequently the problems of adverse selection will be limited. Since the limit values are set at very high levels in some countries, however, the problems associated with adverse selection will probably continue to be a serious issue.

3.4   How can regulation be justified?

In the light of the consequences of regulation it is important to examine the arguments submitted in its support. It appears that regulation has been prompted partly by the requirements of solidarity among different policy-holders (section 3.4.1), and partly by the need to protect the personal integrity of policy-holders (section 3.4.2). Regulation obviously entails treating genetic information differently from other medical information. The reasons in support of this are discussed in section 3.4.3.[29]

3.4.1   Solidarity

If insurance companies are given access to genetic information, discrimination on the basis of the policy-holder's genetic traits is made possible (Skr 1998/99:136, p. 20; Ds 1996:13; NOU 1991:6, p. 131). Persons with increased risks of disease or premature death will be separated from the remaining policy-holders when different risk groups are categorised. In the case of insurance against sickness or premature death, these individuals will normally be debited higher premiums than the remaining policy-holders. And those who run the highest risk of being afflicted by premature death or disease will not be able to obtain insurance at all. In the case of pension insurance without survivor's cover, the situation will be reversed. Those whose genetic traits make premature death highly possible will be offered insurance on particularly favourable terms. It has thus been argued in support of regulation that categorising different risk groups and differentiation of premiums on the basis of genetic information are in conflict with the fundamental idea of insurance and its social goals

---

[29] These and other ethical aspects of insurance companies' access to genetic information are treated in more detail in chapter 7.

(Ot prp nr 49 (1988/89), p. 119, reported in Selmer, 1990, pp. 230 f.). The fundamental idea referred to is apparently that of solidarity (NOU 1991:6, p. 131). What is referred to here, however, is not the basic solidarity between different policy-holders in an insurance collective, where all policy-holders contribute to compensation in loss cases; what seems to be referred to is the solidarity of distribution policy, implying that the cost of the insurance collective's total risk shall be distributed equally, irrespective of the risk status of the individual members of the insurance collective (cf. Radetzki, 1996, p. 247). The regulatory framework thus creates access to insurance cover for groups that would otherwise not be able to obtain insurance.[30]

3.4.2   Integrity and self-determination

Another argument supporting regulation is the view that regulation helps to protect the insurance applicant's personal integrity (Skr 1998/99:136, p. 19; Ds 1996:13, p. 25; NOU 1991:6, p. 131; Folketingstidende, 1996–97, tillægg A, p. 3473). The right to personal integrity entails, among other things, the right to control information about one's own person (Skr 1998/99:136, p. 19; Ds 1996:13, p. 25). However, this right does not encompass all such information, but only information which the majority of citizens in a given society do not wish to be spread (Collste, 1997, p. 794).[31] Even though this does not emerge explicitly, it seems that regulation is based on the conviction that the majority of citizens do not wish information concerning their genetic make-up to be disseminated. Each individual is thus regarded as having the right to genetic integrity (Skr 1998/99:136, p. 19; Ds 1996:13, p. 25). In any case, genetic integrity requires that two basic criteria be satisfied. In the first place each individual is considered to have the right to decide whether a genetic test shall be performed or not (Skr 1998/99:136, p. 19; Ds 1996:13, pp. 25 f.; Folketingstidende, 1996–97, tillægg A, p. 3473): nobody is to be forced to confront information about his future diseases against his will. In the second place, each individual is considered to have the right to know the results of any genetic tests that he may undergo (Skr 1998/99:136, p. 19; Ds 1996:13, p. 26).

---

[30] In a wider perspective the regulatory framework in question could be said to constitute a barrier to the coming into being of a genetic lower class (cf. Sandberg, 2000, pp. 1 f.).

[31] The significance of the concept can vary over time. Conduct which is considered to be prejudicial to an individual's integrity at a certain point in time may become so widely accepted that it will no longer be judged as such. Asking for personal identity (social security in the US) numbers in different contexts may be a good example of this.

The intention thus seems to be some kind of principle of self-determination (Skr 1998/99:136, p. 19; Ds 1996:13, p. 25). In formal terms, such a principle may be considered already to apply without restriction as regards the access of insurance companies to genetic information. As far as is known there are no provisions stipulating that people can be compelled to undergo genetic testing. Furthermore, currently applicable confidentiality provisions probably ensure that each individual who has undergone genetic testing has sole control over the results (Ortner, 2001, p. 15 (regarding Swedish law)).[32] If an insurance applicant undergoes genetic testing or submits available genetic test results, this is done voluntarily and in accordance with the principle of self-determination. This being so, regulation might be considered unnecessary. On the other hand it has been argued that if an insurance applicant perceives the insurance product in question to be vital for his welfare, and the insurance company is willing to provide insurance only to those who submit genetic information, the freedom of self-determination may be illusory (Skr 1998/99:136, p. 20; Ds 1996:13, p. 26; cf. NOU 1991:6, pp. 131 f.).

3.4.3   Should genetic information be treated in a special way?

Both arguments presented above supporting restrictions on insurance companies' access to genetic information are of a general nature and may therefore be used to support the view that restrictions ought to be introduced regarding access to all types of medical information. The question that arises is whether it is correct to treat genetic information in a special way in this context. Is it reasonable that a person who has learned by means of a genetic test that he represents an increased risk in some respect is allowed not to inform the insurer about it, whereas a person who has received similar information in some other way has to inform the insurer (Flood, 1999, p. 106; cf. Brom, 1991, p. 135; Lemmens and Bahamin, 1998, pp. 175 ff.; Lemmens, 2000, pp. 383 ff.)?

One argument in support of the special treatment of genetic information prevailing today is based on the claim that in contrast to medical information in general, genetic information may reveal not only the symptoms of a disease themselves but also an increased risk of developing symptoms in the future. However, genetic information is not the only source of information that may indicate the risk of developing symptoms

---

[32] One interesting question concerns the issue of whether genetic technology entails possibilities of exceptions to this general rule. For a discussion of this issue, which is not treated in this book, see Wachbroit, 1988, pp. 590 ff.

in the future. Another example is the information that can be obtained by an HIV test, which, contrary to what is widely thought, reveals only an increased risk of developing AIDS (Schatz, 1987, p. 178). Despite this, the access of insurance companies to the results of such tests has not been restricted to any great extent.[33]

Another argument adduced in favour of restrictions on the insurer's access to genetic information is that there is a risk that insurers will place too much reliance on the results of genetic tests (Ds 1996:13, p. 28; Folketingstidende, 1996–97, tillægg A, p. 3473). If insurers were given access to genetic information they might deny insurance cover to persons showing an increased risk of a disease such as cancer, for example, even if the risk increase in question was actually negligible.

This argument has a certain amount of cogency; there is empirical evidence showing that insurance companies often overreact to genetic information.[34] The argument can be refuted, however, by the observations that because of competition, insurance companies have strong reasons to see to it that their risk assessment, on which their whole business hinges, is realistic, and that their evaluation of genetic data will improve as their knowledge of genetics grows. Further, no guarantees exist that insurance companies will not overreact in a similar way to other kinds of medical information, such as, for example, the fact that a person has undergone treatment for cancer in the past.[35]

Other reasons supporting special regulation of genetic information are that, in contrast to medical information in general, genetic information will make it possible to determine the presence of susceptibility to a large

---

[33] This applies, at any rate, to Europe (Sandberg, 1996, p. 74). Restrictions of this kind can be found, however, in the United States (Clifford and Iuculano, 1987, pp. 1814 ff.).

[34] A frequently quoted example is the discrimination against healthy African-American carriers of the sickle-cell trait which took place in the 1960s. This group was considered to be susceptible to sickle-cell anaemia when the sickle-cell trait was inherited from one parent. The trait is recessive, however, and not dangerous, as long as it has not been inherited from both parents. An inadequate knowledge of genetics thus led to overreaction (see, for example, Gostin, 1991, p. 118). In a more recent example in Sweden, children have been denied insurance cover subsequent to amniotic fluid tests showing Klinefelter's syndrome (*Göteborgsposten*, 2001), despite the fact that the syndrome does not lead to any disorders other than infertility and unusual tallness. These two examples show that genetic information may be difficult to interpret, which is why it has induced many debaters to call attention to the problems connected with insurance companies' access to such information (Chadwick and Ngwena, 1995, pp. 123 ff.).

[35] Empirical evidence showing that information other than that applying to insurance applicants' genetic traits can cause overreaction on the part of insurance companies can be found in the field of insurance against loss and damage. When insurance companies were to provide insurance for first-generation jet aircraft, the premium was eight times higher than the premium which appeared later on to be equivalent to the risk costs involved (see Radetzki and Radetzki, 2000, p. 186).

number of diseases.[36] The enormous amount of information that it will be possible to collect with the help of genetics would make the information obtained in this way particularly harmful from the point of view of solidarity and integrity, and this, if nothing else, would justify separate regulation (NOU 1991:6, p. 132).[37] There are strong reasons indicating that the argument is based on a correct assumption. Even though there is still considerable uncertainty, there is much to suggest that genetic information will be more informative in the future than general medical information (cf. Sandberg, 1996, p. 77). Those who are concerned about solidarity from the point of view of equal distribution of benefits in society and wish to protect the insurance applicant's personal integrity may consider restriction of the insurer's access to genetic information to be an effective means of achieving this goal.

Serious criticism of the special treatment of genetic information has been expressed by the Norwegian committee of inquiry which proposed in 2000 that genetic information should be equated with other types of medical information (section 3.2.5). The committee stressed the fact that the question of whether a disease or a predisposition to disease is hereditary or whether it has been acquired in some other way is irrelevant from the point of view of risk. The risk of developing cancer may thus be the same irrespective of whether it is due to the individual's genetic make-up or the fact that the individual has been subjected to radiation. The committee was also critical of the view invoked from time to time that genetic information is particularly sensitive, since it concerns not only the individual personally but also his family, and therefore necessitates special treatment. Not only genetic information but other types of information concerning risk factors linked, for example, to housing or working conditions, can tell us something about the individual's health risks. Furthermore, it has been maintained that genetic information is special in that it can identify risks of future diseases before the appearance of any symptoms. In the view of the committee it is difficult to see why symptoms should be perceived as decisive for the evaluation of risk, when this can be evaluated in other ways. Factors other than disease, such as, for example, gender, have been used for a long time to estimate the life expectancy of individuals. Further, in the opinion of the committee, the possibility that people will refrain from otherwise well-motivated

---

[36] As can be seen from section 2.2, approximately 8,000 monogenetic diseases have been identified at the present time. In addition, a number of diseases have been identified that are only partly linked to genetic make-up. The total number of such diseases is unknown but is probably very high.

[37] Note that the pronouncement was made more than ten years ago. Some of the possibilities that could only be anticipated then are now a reality.

genetic tests due to a fear of being denied insurance cover does not mean that genetic information should receive special treatment either. A simple visit to a doctor may reveal risks to health that may have consequences for obtaining insurance (NOU 2000:23, pp. 69 f.).

3.5   Closing remarks

Our book is largely concerned with the regulation restricting the use of genetic information by insurance companies in different countries. This chapter has examined this regulation, its problematic consequences, and the reasons that have been considered to justify the application of regulation despite the problems involved. Regulation finds expression in international conventions, declarations and recommendations, as well as national legislation and voluntary agreements. In general, existing regulation can be said to prevent insurance companies from requiring that applicants shall undergo genetic tests as a prerequisite for providing insurance. In addition, insurance companies are not allowed to access genetic test information in medical records. In some countries the latter prohibition is an absolute one; in other countries the prohibition applies only to cases when the insured amount is lower than a specially stipulated limit value.

Regulation means that the balance of information between insurers and policy-holders is disturbed. Insurance contracts are thus based on asymmetric information, in consequence of which the insurance business risks being affected by adverse selection. Nevertheless, regulation has been regarded as justifiable for reasons of solidarity among different policy-holders and the insurance applicant's personal integrity.

Part II

Social, economic and legal aspects

4 Social insurance in the modern welfare state: emergence, maturity and partial dismantling

4.1 Introduction

The rapid progress of genetic science has little bearing on the collective and obligatory social insurance systems that have been built up to cover the costs of illness and disability, to assure the household's income levels in the event of the breadwinner's premature death, and to provide for a pension during old age. The reason is that these systems do not differentiate between the insured according to individual risks. The entire collective is provided with the same extent of cover, while premiums and benefits are regularly differentiated on the basis of income not of risk. But circumstances are changing, as the public systems are restructured and partially dismantled. Developments during the 1990s have comprised some privatisation of social insurance, while those parts that remain in the public domain have been individualised and exposed to competition in considerable measure. We claim that, to function properly, the structure that is now evolving will be forced to differentiate the premiums it charges, or the comprehensiveness of cover it offers, in accordance with individual risks. At the same time, genetic science is making progress in strides. As shown in chapter 2, there are still important uncertainties about the ultimate potential of genetics for determining individual insurance risks. In that chapter, therefore, we juxtapose a cautious versus a bold scenario in this regard. But irrespective of which of the two scenarios turns out to be true, it is indisputable that continued progress in genetic science will considerably widen the possibilities of determining individual personal insurance risks, and of differentiating insurance premiums accordingly.

The changes of social insurance arrangements that have already occurred and that can be expected in the relatively near future have important implications of both a commercial and an ethical character, which are dealt with in following chapters. Before we reach that point in our analyses, however, it is appropriate to explore the history and shifting roles of social insurance, and in particular to discuss the current restructuring

Table 4.1. *Public expenditure in OECD countries, as a percentage of GDP*

	1937[a]	1960	1980	1999
Total public expenditure	20.7	25.3	36.6	37.8[c]
United States		*25.2*	*33.5*	*32.7[c]*
Western Europe		*27.5*	*42.6*	*44.5*
Of which social insurance[b]	3.8	6.9	13.7	14.2[c]
United States		*5.3*	*11.4*	*12.6[c]*
Western Europe		*9.8*	*17.0*	*16.8*

[a] Relates to a limited group of OECD countries (the OECD itself came into being in 1961).
[b] Defined for 1937 as 'subsidies and transfers'; other years as 'social security transfers'.
[c] 1998.
Sources: Tanzi and Schuknecht, 1995, pp. 4, 11 (for 1937); OECD, 1983, p. 63 (for 1960 and 1980); OECD, 2001, p. 67 (for 1999).

of this important element in the modern welfare state. In this chapter we adopt a chronological method whereby each section deals with a separate period, analysing what actually occurred and detailing the motivations and reasons for the directions of change. Thus, section 4.2 maps the emergence of social insurance, from the beginning of the twentieth century and until some years after the end of the Second World War, when these insurance systems still constituted a relatively small component of the total economy. In section 4.3 we deal with the consolidation and extraordinary expansion of social insurance from about 1960 and until the mid-1980s. Section 4.4 is devoted to the last two decades of the century. It describes, first, how the growth of social insurance was virtually arrested, and then the deep changes in the system's entire structure that followed in the 1990s.

Our account focuses on the rich market economies around the north Atlantic. Table 4.1 is provided as a frame of reference for the discussion, giving historical figures for the countries of the Organisation for Economic Co-operation and Development (OECD), both of total public expenditure, and of social insurance in particular, all as shares of gross domestic product (GDP). Separate figures are provided for the United States and western Europe.

Clearly, social insurance is not a monolith, and its evolution has taken somewhat different paths in the countries under review. Nevertheless, several key features that distinguish it from private insurance have been common everywhere. Thus the systems have all been motivated by solidarity, they have been characterised by strong collective and mandatory elements, public involvement has been all-inclusive in many cases and predominant in others, and the profit motive has been entirely absent in most cases, or at least strongly subdued.

Throughout, our focus is on public arrangements to provide for the costs of the treatment of illness, and to protect against income shortfalls in the event of poor health or premature death, and during old age. These are the fields likely to be affected by improved genetic insights. Other types of social insurance, such as public provision for unemployment or industrial accidents, are only summarily treated, if at all.

4.2   From a humble beginning around the turn of the century until 1950

The preconditions under which social insurance was born more than 100 years ago comprise (i) growing average income levels in industrialising countries; (ii) the break-up of extended families in rural areas, as labour moved in increasing numbers to seek employment in cities and towns; and (iii) the income insecurity that followed from repeating business cycle crises in the industrial economy (Rimlinger, 1971, p. 177). The turn of the century was a period of dynamic structural change, material, social and intellectual. Poverty came to be regarded from a new perspective (Briggs, 1961, p. 253): material destitution was no longer seen solely as the consequence of the behaviour of poor people; instead it was often regarded as a result of society's failings. The new perspective, in turn, provided support to the view that society had a responsibility for addressing the worst consequences of poverty. At the same time, brisk economic growth made it easier to set aside the resources needed for the purpose.

Around 1900, Sidney and Beatrice Webb in the United Kingdom argued, primarily on altruistic grounds, for public measures to assure everybody of the material minimum required for a civilised life (Briggs, 1961, p. 231), but there were also underlying arguments that extreme poverty could have negative consequences for society as a whole. For example, public involvement in providing minimum health services to the entire population was seen as a measure to reduce the risks of epidemic outbreaks. A number of political initiatives were taken in the following decades to expand and make general the state's social responsibilities. The introduction of universal suffrage clearly speeded up this political process. Thus, the UK government established a non-contributory state pension system in 1908, followed in 1911 by national health and unemployment insurance arrangements (Wilson and MacKay, 1941, chs. II–IV). The Labour Party strongly promoted the view that citizens had not only political, but also social rights, and that society had an irrevocable responsibility to assure adequate means of support in the event of illness or premature death and during old age. The doctrine and practice of social insurance were developed by and large in parallel in several of the rich dominions of what was then the British Empire (Briggs, 1961, p. 244). New Zealand had launched a publicly financed pension system for the poor above 65 years of age in 1898, and Australia followed suit in 1908.

Germany was another front-runner in the social insurance field. Although developments there had a different ideological basis, the end result turned out to be quite similar to that in the British Empire. A socialist ideology provided the underpinnings to the reforms in the United Kingdom, the purpose being to liberate people from economic and political inferiority. In Germany, in contrast, social insurance was launched with the explicit purpose of assuaging dissatisfaction and calming agitation in the poor labouring classes. The reforms aimed at constraining the scope for socialist initiatives and maintaining the status quo, with large class and income differences. The objective of social insurance, in other words, was to create a mood of satisfaction and of acceptance of existing inequalities (Rimlinger, 1971, pp. 112 ff., 339). All this is clearly apparent from the speech to parliament in 1884 by the German Chancellor Bismarck, in which he developed his ideas about a social insurance package with guarantees against income shortfalls, in return for political stability and labour market peace (Krueger, 2000, p. 118). Bismarck's reform proposals were codified during the 1880s in a set of laws concerning mandatory insurance to provide the means of living in the event of illness, accident or invalidity, and during old age (Dawson, 1890, p. 9).

The German initiatives in the field of social insurance had a strong influence on the development in many countries. In the 1890s Belgium and Denmark copied the central parts of the German pension system, and Switzerland was also influenced by the German innovations (Briggs, 1961, p. 247). In Sweden too, the social insurance system was modelled on the German pattern (Junestav, 2001, p. 39). Legislation to institute health insurance was adopted by the Swedish parliament in 1910, decisions on a public pension system followed in 1914, and 1916 saw the establishment of obligatory accident insurance for industrial employees (Royal Social Board, 1938, pp. 113 ff.). These provisions were based on contributions from the insured, but with an important public subsidy element. All of them provided an indisputable *right* to compensation (Berge, 1995, p. 10), as distinct from the earlier systems of relief for the poor, which were mainly based on benevolence.

The German model also spread to the United States, primarily through the establishment in 1906 of the German-inspired 'American Association for Labor Legislation', whose strong lobbying led during the following decade to legislation concerning social insurance, particularly in the fields of health and the labour market (Weaver, 1982, p. 35). The United States has lagged belind Europe from the beginning until the present, both with respect to the point in time when social insurance was established, and to the extent of cover and generosity. Also, the public finance element in the US social insurance system has been less dominant than in most European countries. One explanation for the intercontinental differences could be the strong desire to be self-reliant, common among the new settlers in the United States, while another is the existence of a highly developed private philanthropic tradition. Demographic factors also played a role. Large-scale immigration along with rapid population growth reduced the number of the old relative to the population as a whole; care of the old within the household was facilitated as a result (Teune, 1986, p. 22).

Despite gradually growing ambitions, by the middle of the century social insurance systems still had a somewhat limited reach, and they represented a relatively small component in the GDP of the north Atlantic countries. Altenstetter (1986, pp. 79 ff.) argues that early in the twentieth century the German social insurance systems had only partial cover and low compensation levels, while Rimlinger (1971, pp. 194 f.) puts forward a similar claim for the United States around 1930. Writing about Sweden in 1928, Berge (1995, p. 53) notes that 44.6 per cent of urban pensioners had to rely on relief for the poor, since the pension rights were insufficient to cover the cost of living.

The entire public sector was of quite limited size during the first half of the twentieth century, compared with what was to follow. In 1913, total public expenditure in a group of future OECD countries was assessed at no more than 9 per cent of GDP (13–15 per cent in leading countries such as the United Kingdom and Germany). The cost of the transfers and subsidies comprising the cost of social insurance constituted far less than half of these totals (Tanzi and Schuknecht, 1995, pp. 4, 11). The development of social insurance was strongly boosted by the Great Depression in the early 1930s, particularly in the United States, which was among the hardest hit by economic contraction (Ashford, 1986, pp. 3 f.). Despite this boost, the public cost of social insurance remained at a very modest level. In 1937, expenditure for these purposes was only 2.1 per cent of GDP in the United States, and 3.8 per cent in a group of future OECD countries for which data are available (table 4.1). The explanation of these low levels is that, as noted, until the mid-1950s most social insurance lacked general cover and was primarily a safety net for the poor and most exposed groups.

4.3   Consolidation and the great expansion, 1950–1980

The golden age of social insurance occurred during the decades following the Second World War. Only then were the public income protection systems truly generalised to cover the entire population, with the benefits regarded as inalienable rights. And since the rights had this general character, they gave rise to the view that compensation should be related to average income, a much higher ambition than the former aim to protect against destitution (Berge, 1995, p. 62; Titmuss, 1950, p. 506; Weaver, 1982, pp. 169 ff.). The emerging values gained wide political support, and were reflected in policy formulation and implementation. Thus, for example, while in 1939, the average pension in twelve future OECD countries corresponded to no more than 15.4 per cent of average wages in the relevant groups, by 1980 the corresponding share had risen to 45 per cent (World Bank, 1994, p. 104).

Important consequences for the public budgets soon followed from this change in attitude and in practical policy. As can be seen in table 4.1, total public expenditure in the future OECD countries rose from 20.7 per cent of GDP in 1937 to 25.3 per cent in 1960. From then on, the expansion gained speed, so that by 1980 public expenditure had reached 36.6 per cent of GDP. The public costs of social insurance grew even faster. They almost quadrupled in the period 1937–80 (from 3.8 per cent to 13.7 per cent of GDP), and so completely dominated the overall expansion in public expenditure.

An important background element to the extreme generosity towards the beneficiaries of social insurance was the historically exceptional economic expansion in the rich country group during the third quarter of the twentieth century. Demographic trends also contributed. A fast and steady population growth appeared to be guaranteed by the postwar baby boom. While total GDP expanded at impressive rates on account of ever rising productivity and increasing population numbers, politicians found it both easy and opportune to be generous. It was also easy to ignore the chain-letter features of what went on, with the active generations assuming rapidly expanding responsibilities for the older cohorts (Samuelson, 1967). The pension arrangements were regularly structured as pay-as-you-go systems in which the labour force contributions covered the costs. This choice was no doubt partly explained by the painful experiences of the 1920s and 1930s, when funded pension systems invested in bonds in Germany and Austria, and in shares in the United States, imploded as a consequence of hyper-inflation and depression, respectively. Perhaps a more important reason for the choice of system was that it permitted immediate benefits to new pensioner groups, while the costs of maintaining the system and of repairing its possible deficiencies was pushed on to future generations. The sickness and disability insurance systems were characterised by the same generosity, with very limited control requirements and with small deductibles charged to the beneficiaries.

Prominent academics from the field of economics and other social science disciplines developed sophisticated arguments in favour of the expansion of social insurance. Politicians eagerly absorbed the message, in a desire to catch the votes of additional groups of beneficiaries. Little reflection was given to the longer-term consequences of ongoing developments and to the system's sustainability.

Despite their differences, all the north Atlantic societies that are the focus of our interest are market economies of different shades. A basic perception about such economies is that the motives for public intervention are weak or completely absent as long as the markets function well. In the 1960s and 1970s the study of market failures caught the fancy of many prominent economists. Influential proponents of social insurance established a doctrine which claimed that the markets for personal insurance to cover income loss in the event of illness or premature death and during old age were particularly prone to a variety of failures. The perception that private markets were unable to satisfy such insurance needs became a key motive for continued expansion of social insurance. There is reason to scrutinise the content of this doctrine, especially since a counter-doctrine (see section 4.4) emerged during the 1980s, providing the intellectual underpinnings to the partial dismantling of social insurance systems in the 1990s.

Kenneth Arrow's influential paper from the early 1960s (Arrow, 1963) constituted a central tenet in the doctrine which claimed that the private markets for personal insurance services were deficient. Arrow makes two statements.

The first is that the market for health insurance (and analogously the markets for insurance against premature death and for pensions) is characterised by incomplete information (pp. 945 f.), for example where the insured knows more than the insurer about the risks being covered. This asymmetric information in turn leads to adverse selection, where insurance holders who know that they represent only limited risks tend to refrain from purchasing insurance, because they feel, correctly, that they are charged premiums which are higher than would be stipulated by an appropriate actuarial assessment. The end result of the tendency towards accentuated adverse selection would be the collapse of the private insurance market.[1] Arrow argues that as societies perceive the deficiencies of specific markets, they tend to set up non-market institutions to compensate for the emerging shortcomings. Collective and mandatory social insurance systems, one of the main pillars of the welfare state, are examples. Such systems have been set up to cover a need that private markets do not easily satisfy. Arrow reasoned that social insurance established by the welfare state provides a supply to satisfy an existing demand, thereby contributing to higher social welfare levels (Barr, 1992, p. 795).

Arrow's second argument is that mandatory social insurance whose cover and premium payments are unrelated to individual risks is an efficient instrument for redistribution in favour of the least endowed within the collective (Arrow, 1963, p. 947). The group which for various reasons represents a high insurance risk will be compensated by the low-risk ones in a solidarist arrangement where neither the extent of benefits nor premium levels depend on risk. To the extent that risk differences can be established *ex ante*, social insurance will not be actuarially based, at least not in the short run. The high-risk groups pay too little, and the low-risk ones too much, but this is precisely the purpose of the arrangement. The redistribution in favour of the unfortunates is a component built into the system for the purpose of reducing social inequalities.

Arrow also maintains that the redistribution and the neglect of actuarial principles are only apparent, a result of the observer's myopia. If social insurance is viewed in a longer and broader perspective, where those to be insured have not yet been born, and hence different risk groups cannot be identified, then obviously the premiums cannot be related to risk. The average premium must nevertheless be set at a level that covers the cost of the entire insured collective, for otherwise the system will not be sustainable in the long run. With this viewpoint, social insurance appears as clearly actuarial, and its role as an instrument for redistribution loses significance (p. 964). Here it would appear that Arrow anticipates Rawls's (1972) famous 'veil of ignorance'.[2] The welfare state as a whole can be regarded as a gigantic and voluntary insurance contract in this perspective

[1] Arrow was clearly on the right track, but his conclusions were premature. Empirical investigations of adverse selection show that his fears were exaggerated. The extent of asymmetric information has not been sufficiently marked to threaten private insurance markets with collapse. But the threats that Arrow pointed to are bound to become much more serious once further progress in genetic science increases the scope for risk assessment, while at the same time the insurance companies are denied access to the results of genetic tests (chs. 3 and 5).

[2] Rawls's argument runs as follows. Let us determine the desirable social contract while we remain behind the veil of ignorance concerning our own position in society (for instance because we have not yet been born). Since there is a possibility that we will end up in the least fortunate group, we will tend to choose arrangements that favour that group, as

(Barr, 1992, p. 795). The efficiency gain following from the satisfaction of a demand that markets find hard to handle is only an additional bonus.

Another failing frequently put forward is the inability of funded private pension systems to protect their clients against unexpected inflation (Barr, 1992, pp. 768 f.; Gordon, 1988, p. 169). Private pension funds provide 'protection' against the possibility of a long life, by having those who die early subsidise those who die late. But such funds are unable to protect against the risk that inflation depletes the value of the fund's overall assets, and the depletion has to be borne by the entire collective of insured. The same must be true for a stock exchange collapse. As noted earlier in the chapter, this is precisely what happened to the pension funds invested in Austrian and German bonds, and in American stock during the crises of the 1920s and 1930s. In this light, the observation that hardly any of the existing private pension systems in the United States provide protection against inflation (Bodie, 1990, p. 36) is not surprising. Since private markets have failed in protecting against such risks, the main responsibility for their handling has been taken over by the public institutions of the welfare state.

Those who developed the doctrine described in the preceding paragraphs openly admit that the collective elements of social insurance constrain individuals' freedom of action. But they also argue that this disadvantage must be weighed against the private markets' inability to deliver (Inman, 1987, pp. 692, 755). The democratic societies in western Europe made a conscious choice during the decades after the Second World War in favour of the solidarist welfare state, with its ensuing restrictions on individual freedom. The choice went in the same direction in the United States too (Weaver, 1982, ch. 8), even though it was less marked than in western Europe. The US system comprises an array of social insurances as comprehensive as those in western Europe, but private elements in the system are more common, while compensation levels and costs have remained lower, at least in relative terms.

4.4   Re-evaluation and restructuring after 1980

A clear shift in the trend of fast growing costs for social insurance occurred in the early 1980s. Between 1960 and 1980, the share of social insurance expenditures rose from 6.9 per cent to 13.7 per cent of GDP in the OECD countries, or by a total of 6.8 percentage points. During the following

---

for instance in the collective, obligatory social insurance systems, where the unfortunate are not required to pay higher premiums on account of the high insurance risks that they may represent.

nineteen years the costs increased further, to 14.2 per cent of GDP, a mere 0.5 percentage points. Table 4.1 demonstrates that the expansion was greater in western Europe during both periods, but the change in trend is equally evident on both sides of the Atlantic. In fact, the west European social insurance transfers peaked in 1983, at 18.3 per cent of GDP, and fell thereafter, to 16.8 per cent in 1999. In absolute numbers, the shift was even more pronounced, for while the OECD's total GDP rose by more than 4 per cent a year in the period 1960–80, the growth rate in the subsequent period was only 2.6 per cent (OECD, 2001, p. 48).

The shift has had two causes, which both led to disillusion with the existing arrangements. The first was practical. The strong expansion of the costs of social insurance resulted in rising concerns and problems with financing the public commitments. The second was more fundamental, and involved a radical re-evaluation of the utility of social insurance, and of the need for deep public involvement in the field. A set of systemic shortcomings in the social insurance system, akin to the private market failures discussed above, gradually came to the fore.

4.4.1   Practical problems

Social insurance systems were expanded in the 1950s and 1960s under the presumption of continuously growing population and income levels. The rules were made generous, since it was generally believed that the rising costs would easily be absorbed in an expanding GDP. This presumption has proved erroneous (World Bank, 1994, p. 105): during the fourth quarter of the twentieth century, population numbers stagnated in the countries under review, and the growth of productivity experienced a sharp decline. The rate of overall economic expansion, therefore, turned out to be much less dynamic than earlier expectations.

With low economic growth since the mid-1970s and tax rates already established at elevated levels to finance the very ambitious state budgets of the OECD countries, politicians found it increasingly difficult to raise public revenue to even higher levels in order to finance the ongoing expenditure increases. Rising budget deficits followed, and with them increasing public indebtedness, whose speed and magnitude exceeded anything recorded until then during peace time (Masson and Mussa, 1995, p. 1). The developments were clearly not sustainable. Radical reforms of social insurance were seen as the obvious remedy, given that the social insurance system accounted for a dominant share of the growth in public expenditure.

The need to change public pension systems appeared to be particularly pertinent. As noted, these systems were based on the *pay-as-you-go* model, where each active generation is expected to finance the income maintenance of the old. With rising average life expectancy and elaborate arrangements to secure the incomes of individuals who chose or were forced to retire before the standard pension age, the burden of pension payments has become increasingly onerous for the labour force. In the 1980s the World Bank assessed the remaining life expectancy for those in the rich countries reaching the formal retirement age at fourteen to eighteen years for men and seventeen to twenty-three years for women (World Bank, 1994, p. 371), up from only a couple of years early in the century (Weaver, 1982, p. 33). In reality, the expected duration of retirement was even longer, given the widespread practice of an early departure from working life. The present cost of the implicit public obligation for future pension payments has been estimated at more than three times current GDP in France, Italy and Germany, among others (Masson and Mussa, 1995, p. 22), a sum several times greater than the overall public debt, traditionally calculated. Future generations have to bear the consequences of these arrangements.

Three circumstances have contributed to the explosive developments in costs of public health care, and all three have become kick-off points for the subsequent reforms. (i) Very generous rules, for example no deductibles for the insured, weak control of benefit payments and an increasingly firm attitude that the benefits were inalienable rights (Masson and Mussa, 1995, p. 9), led to a situation where ever larger groups claimed compensation for illness or invalidity, or an early pension, even where the true reasons for making the claims were ambiguous and weak (Lindbeck, 1995, p. 11).[3] (ii) Technological progress in the medical field has given rise to new treatment methods, some of which are extremely expensive. In the same line as pointed to by Lindbeck above, decision-makers in the medical profession and in the public health insurance bodies have experienced serious difficulties in denying the use of these treatments, even when their utility was deemed as highly marginal. (iii) The demographic factor has also played a role. With low birth rates and extended longevity,

---

[3] Isaksson provides an interesting example from Sweden of the way in which the rules were stretched and the costs expanded. In the 1970s the government introduced sixty days' publicly paid maternity leave (substantially expanded in later years), to compensate women who were too tired to work late into their pregnancy. Since the rules permitted the women to avail themselves of the benefit both before and after childbirth, increasing numbers of pregnant women chose to take paid sick leave late during pregnancy, and to use the maternity compensation in its entirety after birth, thereby increasing the total publicly paid leave in a manner not intended by the legislator. This adjustment has subsequently developed into an accepted norm. Around the turn of the century, about 80 per cent of pregnant women have taken sick leave of two to three months before birth (Isaksson, 2001, p. 36).

the proportion of the old in the total population has risen. Since the need for medical services is highest during old age, the result has been a steep increase in the cost of health maintenance and care.

4.4.2   Fundamental dilemmas caused by social insurance

Solidarity was the guiding line when social insurance was originally established. As long as poverty was acute and common, it was easy to muster ethical arguments in favour of income protection when income loss was caused by circumstances beyond the individual's control. Solidarity with the needy overrode the disadvantage of the constraints on individual freedom that followed from public undertakings under those conditions. In the prosperity characterising the north Atlantic countries during the last two decades of the twentieth century, the poorest groups were not at all as poor as in earlier periods, and the need for safety nets is far less critical.

Offers of expanded social insurance have come to be used by governments and their political opposition in attempts to win elections. Political parties have outbid each other in their promises, in efforts to make their respective programmes look attractive to voters. Such political behaviour has resulted in an uncontrolled increase in expenditure in many cases, with ensuing budget crises as a consequence (Weaver, 1982, pp. 124, 169 f.).

The bodies that supplied social insurance have all had monopolistic features, and many have been outright monopolies. Characteristics such as an opaque principal–agent relationship, with unclear distribution of responsibilities between the bureaucrats and their political masters, absence of incentives to minimise costs for a given volume of services, and inability to cater to individual wishes and needs (Barr, 1992, p. 790), have come to appear as increasingly serious shortcomings in the existing arrangements.

Some economic activities (e.g. mining, steel production or forest exploitation) carry greater risks of sickness and accident than others (telecom production, computer programming). The former, therefore, impose a higher cost for health and rehabilitation than the latter. Undifferentiated charges for public health insurance involve a subsidy to strenuous and risky endeavours, since the charges imposed on them do not cover the full costs that they generate.[4] The ensuing structural bias in favour of heavy industry is hard to justify, and has been seen as yet another deficiency of the social insurance structure (Hansson, Lyttkens and Skogh, 1984, pp. 23 ff.).

---

[4] Industrial accident insurance schemes in some countries, e.g. France, Germany and the United States, do differentiate premiums by industry branch.

The mature social insurance system presents something of a paradox in the modern market economy. As is apparent from section 4.3, the system was established to overcome the shortcomings of private insurance markets, particularly the supposed inability of such markets to protect against macroeconomic shocks such as unexpected inflation or collapses on stock exchanges. Ironically, however, large and mature social insurance arrangements themselves create risks of similar macroeconomic shocks. It is evident that governments facing unmanageable budget deficits may be forced to implement severe cuts in their expenditure streams, including social insurance payments, and these will obviously strike at the clients of social insurance (Lindbeck, 1995, pp. 13 f.). This is precisely what happened in Sweden and Finland in the early 1990s. Thus, the deficiencies of private markets are simply replaced by the risks of unanticipated change in the politically determined system of rules. It is by no means clear which of the two shortcomings is the more serious.

One must also note that the beneficiaries of social insurance are not alone in suffering from a system under disintegration. Social insurance protection against income shortfalls has been widely regarded as a macroeconomic stabiliser, helping to maintain economic activity during recessions. More recently this advantage has been put in serious doubt (Lindbeck, 1995, pp. 11 f.). If the government is forced to save, and to cut social insurance payments precisely during a recession when its revenues decline, the consequence will be an accentuation of the business cycle decline, which could well develop into macroeconomic collapse. Experiences in Sweden and Finland during the early 1990s provide examples of an overgrown social insurance system that the government could no longer afford becoming a macroeconomic destabiliser.

4.4.3   The content of the reforms

In sum, the disillusion with social insurance, based both on practical experiences and more fundamental considerations, has led to a far-reaching re-evaluation of the existing systems. This, in turn, has prompted the reforms that have characterised the developments during the 1990s.

Kotlikoff's assertion that 'privatisation of social insurance is spreading throughout the world' (Kotlikoff, 1996, pp. 1 ff.) is of course both an exaggeration and oversimplification. Nevertheless, it is clear that social insurance has been subjected to thorough reforms in a number of OECD countries in the course of the 1990s (OECD, 1998, p. 53). These reforms had at least three objectives. The first and most important has been to limit the state's involvement, and to stabilise and reduce its expenditure streams in this area. The second aimed at making the existing systems more efficient by clarifying the applicable rules, improving and expanding controls, raising deductibles, and in many cases by exposing the systems to competition. The *third* involved measures to increase the freedom of choice, and so to make it easier to satisfy specific individual needs. The whole reform package can of course be referred to as 'privatisation', as Kotlikoff has done, if this term is juxtaposed to 'socialisation' (Söderström *et al.*, 2001, p. 9), but it is readily apparent from what follows that the process of change has been much more complex.

The content of reforms as well as their speed has varied among the countries, but the following elements are found in almost all cases:

- Commercialisation and increased sensitivity to individual needs. Examples comprise exposure of the public service supply to competition, for instance in health care, where former state monopolies have to compete for their clients, sometimes among themselves, for example across administrative boundaries, in other cases with newly established private health service suppliers, all with the aim of reducing costs and/or improving quality; the establishment of separate pension accounts with the state pension authority, where the individual can himself decide how the funds should be invested; rising contributions by the individual, or his employer in some cases, to reduce the complete dominance of the public finance component; greater scope for the individual to determine the amount of premium payments and level of the ensuing benefits.

- Reduced public generosity towards the insured. Examples include stricter criteria for compensation for sickness and invalidity, and for pension payments before the standard pensionable age; more detailed control of individual cases before payment is executed; increased deductibles; falling real compensation levels in consequence of an unwillingness to index the social insurance payments to rising labour incomes or to inflation.

- Encouragement to supplement or replace social insurance with private alternatives. Such encouragement is the direct corollary of lesser public generosity. Where the extent of the public safety net is reduced, it is natural for many individuals to undertake their own compensatory measures. Adjustments in the tax rules for the precise purpose of making private supplements to social insurance more attractive, have been common. In some cases, opt-out offers have been opened up, permitting the individual to leave social insurance altogether, and to replace it with private arrangements.

Political opposition to the reforms from many groups has been quite strong (Tanzi and Schuknecht, 1995, p. 27). This has reduced the pace of change, and the reform process is far from complete. Events in Germany provide examples of recently initiated change still under implementation. Thus, in the course of 2000, a political agreement was reached to expand the pension system through a private superstructure on the public system. Additionally, in 2001, the Social Democrat economy minister launched a proposal that employers' contributions to health insurance should be spent on financing the employees' private health plans. German trade unions have slowed the progress of these reforms by their sharp criticisms and assertions that the proposed reforms deplete the solidarity inherent in social insurance (*Financial Times*, 2001, p. 2).

Developments like these are not unique to Germany. Commercialisation of the social insurance systems and adjustment to individual needs will no doubt continue, despite the opposition from those who dislike the reforms. Private alternatives are likely to gain expanding roles, primarily in consequence of the practical problems and fundamental dilemmas arising from social insurance.

Important implications follow from the ongoing change for the themes developed in our book. With a full-fledged, comprehensive and mandatory social insurance system in force, commercially oriented insurance in the health, premature death and pension fields constituted to most a relatively marginal good of a luxury character. Private personal insurance changes character as public systems are dismantled and suppressed. Such insurance will then become a good of vital significance to the individual's welfare, and the conditions of access to this good will become an increasingly important social concern.

We have shown in chapter 3 that differentiation of premiums based on individual risk assessments provides a competitive advantage to commercial insurance activities. The survival of private insurance firms that fail to employ this advantage is threatened. The same is true for the public but commercialised organisations that are partly replacing the traditional social insurance suppliers. Both types of individual personal insurance providers must take account of the risk profiles of discrete groups of clients, and ultimately of individuals, if they are to function well. The assessment of risk, in turn, will lead to actuarially based premium differentiation, and an unwillingness to accept certain risks altogether. This involves an important deviation from traditional social insurance, where solidarity reigns and risk differences do not influence the level of premium payments. Differentiation, either of premiums, or of the extent of benefits, will be widened on the basis of risk, to a certain extent today, but possibly quite a lot in the future, if the insurers are allowed to use genetic insights for risk assessment. This raises important social and ethical issues that need to be addressed by the welfare state political systems.

5 International trade in personal insurance

5.1 Introduction

In chapter 3 we described the existing restrictions against the use of genetic information for the purpose of establishing insurance contracts in the north Atlantic countries. In this and the next chapter we question the sustainability of these restrictions. Thus the present chapter analyses how international trade in personal insurance could undermine the existing national regulations. Chapter 6 points to the fact that these regulations do not rest on a legally coherent and uniform ground, and that therefore there are no principal reasons why they should remain in their present form if it turns out, as we claim, that they do not satisfy the ends for which they were initially set up.

Our discussion in the present chapter has been structured as follows. In section 5.2 we describe the deepening internationalisation that has characterised global economic development during the past several decades. In addition, we briefly explore the triggers behind and consequences of the international integration trends. Section 5.3 points to the commercial niche that is being established as a result of the existing prohibitions in an increasing number of countries against the use of genetic information in insurance. We also make an assessment of the importance of this niche under a variety of circumstances, in particular to establish whether there are sufficient incentives for individuals to seek insurance outside the reach of the regulating authorities. Section 5.4 examines the ultimate consequences of international trade, and concludes that the existing prohibitions against the use of genetic information will be hard to sustain in a longer time perspective, and also that they will ultimately prove not to be very meaningful. On these grounds, we argue that the prohibitions will be repealed.

5.2 The deepened integration of the world economy

It is easy to demonstrate the speedy integration of the world's rich economies during the most recent decades. In 1970, the weighted average of combined imports and exports of goods and services of the rich countries (the great majority of which constitute the OECD member states) was 28 per cent of their GDP (World Bank, 1995, pp. 167, 187). By 1998 that share had risen to 45 per cent (World Bank 2000a, pp. 231, 269). Not only trade has been intensified – capital too, has become much more mobile. In 1987, the weighted average of the rich countries' total cross-border flows of portfolio investments[1] was 7 per cent of their GDP, while average direct foreign investments added another 1.5 per cent to the total. In 1999, only twelve years later, the volume of these flows had doubled, to average 14.5 per cent and 3.8 per cent respectively (World Bank, 1999, p. 326; World Bank, 2000b, p. 316). International tourism has experienced an explosive growth, and this, in turn, has contributed to cultural diversification. Peruvian street musicians, Indian classical dance in the concert hall and sushi instead of steak and chips in the restaurant, all once rare phenomena in most west European countries, have become commonplace.

The increasing openness towards the rest of the world has been promoted by far-reaching deregulation in many areas, primarily, but by no means exclusively, in the rich world. Anti-trust legislation has been sharpened, reducing the scope for monopolistic exploitation. State-owned giants in 'sectors of particular importance to the national interest', such as steel, power or uranium enrichment, have been privatised, sometimes even sold to foreign owners. The quest for profitability has resulted in closures of domestic production facilities that could not stand up to international competition, and the supply from such facilities has been replaced by imports. Trade barriers have been reduced in rich as well as poor countries, and the foreign trade bureaucracy has been both suppressed and streamlined. Multinational corporations thrive in the new environment. More positive attitudes towards foreign direct investments have made it easier than ever before to establish export-oriented production of goods and services even in 'far-away' countries such as Bangladesh or Indonesia.

Declining costs of transport and communication have constituted another prime mover towards intensified internationalisation (Lundgren, 1996). By the 1990s the cost of air freight had fallen to less than half that in the 1960s; the cost of telecommunications had declined by more than 90 per cent in the corresponding period. Geographical monopolies have virtually disappeared in consequence. The development of the Internet and e-trade are also contributing to global integration, but this technological jump is so recent that its ultimate consequences are still

---

[1] Investments in bonds and in shares without a claim on corporate control.

hard to judge. Producers of goods and services have greater scope than ever before to split up their production processes into discrete stages, and to transfer each to the location that offers the greatest advantage in terms of costs. This possibility has at the same time become a requirement, for without such adjustment, firms risk being eliminated by more flexible competitors.

From the consumer's point of view, the international economic integration has in many respects erased national borders. Ericsson, the global telecommunications equipment giant, is widely regarded as a Swedish company, Nokia, its competitor, as a Finnish one. But is a mobile telephone from Ericsson more Swedish than one from Nokia, when international pension funds dominate both companies' ownership, and when most of their production facilities have been located outside Scandinavia?

One may rightly wonder about the production venue of a financial service marketed by the local bank, recently integrated with an international financial group, when visits to the bank branch have been replaced by Internet services or contacts with a call centre, located heaven knows where, but whose agents speak the local language with an impeccable accent. Language barriers are losing their importance for cross-border commercial relations, both because the suppliers adjust their marketing efforts to national conditions, and because of improving language skills among consumers. Computerised translation and interpretation can be expected to reduce further the significance of language barriers in the foreseeable future.

The 'home' of electronic trade is ambiguous, and in fact not very important, so long as the trade mark is well known, and faith in the supplier's ability to live up to his commitments not in question. In the world of the early twenty-first century, consumers feel much more at home with the supply of foreign goods and services than ever before, to the extent that they can at all distinguish them from domestic ones. This tendency is of course much more accentuated among younger generations which have grown up in this new environment.

For the purpose of our investigations, it would have been particularly useful to indicate the internationalisation of the insurance business. Unfortunately, there are only scattered, and not very reliable, data on this phenomenon. Insurance, like many other services, has traditionally been subject to substantial discriminatory practices and trade barriers, aimed at protecting domestic business. In 1993, however, a new multilateral agreement on trade in services was adopted under the auspices of the General Agreement on Tariffs and Trade (GATT), providing a valuable framework for liberalisation of services in general, including the foreign activities of insurance companies. Significant progress on liberalisation

Table 5.1. *Foreign insurance companies' market share (gross premium) in the domestic market*

	1985	1993 %	2000
Life			
Denmark	8	8	15
Germany	7[a]	11	15
Netherlands	21	23	32[e]
Norway	0	2	14
Japan	1	3	10
United States	9[b]	15	22
Non-life			
Denmark	14	37	43
Germany	8[a]	14[c]	13
Netherlands	25	26	36
Norway	1	19[d]	47
Japan	3	3	26
United States	7[b]	10	12

[a] 1986. [b] 1990. [c] 1992. [d] 1996. [e] 1999.
Source: OECD, annual: 1993; 2002.

has since then been accomplished within the OECD area. Intra-European and transatlantic mergers have played an important role in the industry's restructuring in the late 1990s. For instance, in 1999, the Dutch group Aegon became the third largest life insurer in the United States through acquisitions. In the same year, German insurer Allianz took a controlling interest in South Korea's fourth largest life insurer, and bought two companies in Taiwan. In contrast, the initial achievements in the rest of the world have been disappointing (*Insurance in Europe*, 1996, pp. 25 ff.; 1999, p. 11). The OECD secretariat publishes foreign insurance companies' market share, measured as gross premium, in the domestic markets of some countries (OECD, annual, 1993; 2002). This, of course, is not the same as international trade, as traditionally defined. Nevertheless, the numbers in table 5.1 do provide support for an intensifying internationalisation trend in the insurance business.

Globalisation is reducing the scope of independent action in an increasing number of areas for national authorities desirous to establish regulation and maintain control in a variety of fields. In the 1960s, when abortion was generally prohibited in most of Europe, national authorities made vain efforts to criminalise women who had abortions performed in Poland, where it was legal. Similarly, in the 1970s, the authorities in several European countries bent on control of the sources of culture, seriously planned prohibitions of television satellite dishes, which at that time had their commercial breakthrough. Such national interventions have become virtually impossible after the waves of internationalisation that have since swept the world. Abortion laws have been liberalised in most of Europe, and prohibitions against satellite dishes are nowadays maintained only by extreme dictatorial regimes. Legislative proposals in the United States in 2002 to forbid therapeutic cloning (using cloned embryos to extract stem cells) aimed at providing cures for genetic diseases such as diabetes or Parkinson's disease, do not even consider the possibility of prosecuting Americans who would undergo such treatment in countries outside the United States where such measures are legal (*The Economist*, 2002a, pp. 45 f.).

Enterprises, but increasingly also individuals, are becoming geographically more mobile, and their true domicile is becoming blurred. This makes it increasingly difficult to maintain national taxation that deviates significantly from the rest of the world. Three examples, of relevance for the central issue in this book, illustrate possible ways of avoiding taxation as well as other government controls by location outside a national authority's reach. All three relate to services akin to those produced by insurance companies. All three contain ethical considerations. The first two relate to tax planning that does not appear to break any law, while the third involves clear-cut tax fraud. The first two also demonstrate that governments are willing to reconsider legislation in the face of international developments that make it ineffective and/or counterproductive.

The first example relates to the betting industry in the United Kingdom, an activity that many regard as morally dubious. In the 1990s the UK government, prompted by both ethical and fiscal considerations, imposed a tax on the turnover of this activity (*The Economist*, 2000, p. 13). The result of the fiscal imposition was that the firms involved in this trade quickly established subsidiaries in low tax countries, from which they carried on an increasing proportion of their business. Customers, predominantly, but in no way exclusively, from the United Kingdom, could place their bets twenty-four hours a day, by telephone or through the internet. Some of the firms found the offshore activity so convenient that they moved all their business to the new locations. The ability of the UK government to intervene has been quite limited, and focused initially on restrictions against advertising the new services in the UK media. Clients from the United States, where betting is strictly regulated, and prohibited outright in some states, were provided with opportunities to avoid the restrictive US legislation by opening accounts directly with the offshore firms. Such arrangements did not violate any legislation in the United Kingdom, and it is not apparent that they infringed any US laws. In 2001, the UK government, pragmatically, eliminated the tax on turnover as a first step in a general liberalisation of betting, reflecting both a desire to recoup lost corporate taxes on the betting enterprises, and a shift of moral attitudes in favour of betting. A number of the Internet bookmakers transferred their business back to the United Kingdom in consequence (*The Economist*, 2002b, pp. 26 f.).

The second example relates to a turnover tax on stock exchange transactions introduced by the Swedish government in 1987 (Eklund, 1998, pp. 39 f.). The motive for the tax was not primarily to generate revenue, but political and moral: the Social Democrat government considered the excessive profits and wages in the financial sector to be unjust. Hence it was felt that profits should be cut, and the ensuing public revenue used for more worthy purposes. Although Sweden at the time still had highly restrictive currency regulations, the actors found means to move a very large part in the securities trade from Stockholm to London. The consequence was far smaller fiscal revenues than the authorities had expected, and a deterioration in the functioning of the stock market on account of a dramatically lowered liquidity. The latter consequence was, of course by far the more important, and the tax did not survive for long.

The third example relates to taxation of interest income in Germany (*The Economist*, 2000, p. 17; Eklund, 1998, p. 43). To ensure tax revenues from a source that is hard to control and often left undeclared, the German authorities introduced in 1993 a 30 per cent tax at source on interest paid to individuals liable to tax in the country. The result was a massive flight of savings from Germany, primarily to Luxembourg and Switzerland, where foreign-owned savings are not taxed and bank secrecy is tight. According to the German Bundesbank's assessments, German tax has subsequently been paid on only one-fifth of the interest payments on German household savings.

The obedience of national tax rules is not likely to be much improved as a result of intergovernmental collaboration, for instance at European Union level, as long as there are countries somewhere in the world, with a good reputation and reliable institutions, which choose to stay out of such collaboration.

The German problem in taxing household savings has more recently been elevated to a European Union (EU) issue, with all member governments wishing to exact dues on their nationals' interest income. But there are deep divisions on the methods to be used. The UK government refuses to impose a general withholding tax because it feels that the London financial market would lose competitive strength in the process. The governments of Luxembourg, Austria and Belgium are unwilling to relax their banking secrecy legislation, and to provide information to foreign tax authorities, for fear of losing a profitable business (*Financial Times*, 2002, p. 3). Writing in the same issue of the *Financial Times* (p. 13), Frits Bolkestein, the European Commissioner for taxation, suggests that 'some of those [countries within the EU] calling for the strongest possible measures to fight the evasion of savings tax are doing so in the hope that by setting the standards unrealistically high, they will wreck the whole enterprise'. Even if all EU members were to agree on the rules to be followed, capital could flee to countries outside the EU, notably Switzerland and the United States. Despite considerable prodding by EU politicians and bureaucrats, the administrations of the two countries have steadfastly refused to co-operate with the European initiatives for information sharing (*The Economist*, 2002c, p. 86). An effective accord continues to be elusive.

Vito Tanzi (2001, pp. 34 ff.) expressively describes a long row of 'fiscal termites' that thrive in the internationally integrated environment, and that chew into the national fiscal bases until only the crust is left. As the reach of national fiscal legislation becomes more and more vague in an economically integrating world, the difficulties in clarifying who is liable to tax, who has the authority to collect the revenue, and to whom it is ultimately destined to go, are continuously being augmented. Swedish purchases of books via the Internet from Amazon.com in Germany illustrate the haze referred to by Tanzi. In principle, but maybe not in practice, such a purchase is subject to value added tax. But is German or Swedish tax applicable? Should Amazon or the customs authorities (as long as these authorities retain any authority for controlling internal trade within the EU) collect the tax, or should the buyer himself declare the transaction and pay the dues? The muddiness is substantial, and in its wake, the possibility of avoiding the tax altogether is considerable.

The conclusions of this discussion, with a direct bearing on our main theme, are easy to summarise. The world economy is speedily integrating. The replacement of lazy monopolies by competitive conditions in a variety of markets forces firms to keep costs down if they are to survive. Consumers find it increasingly hard to distinguish between goods and services that have been produced at home and elsewhere. Trusted trade marks are becoming more important than geographical origin as a guarantee of quality. National regulations are ever harder to enforce if they differ from conditions elsewhere. The scope for differential taxation is being undermined by the increasing possibility of moving production or consumption outside the national fiscal authorities' control. International collaboration between regulators or tax authorities remains ineffective as long as a trustworthy country decides to stay out. Since a country's decision to refrain from such collaboration is likely to enhance its international competitiveness greatly, we deem it improbable that a global agreement on tax co-operation, or on any other similar issue, involving all the world's countries could be brought about.

5.3 Personal insurance based on genetic information: a niche for the insurance industry

5.3.1 Basic preconditions

Commercially oriented insurance activities that are not subject to restrictions on the use of genetic information will clearly reap a competitive advantage in relation to insurance firms subject to restrictions in this field (chapter 3). The deepening integration of the world economy expands the possibilities of benefiting from this competitive advantage. Two preconditions must prevail for a significant niche to arise.

The first is that the progress of genetic science will in fact make it possible to separate insurance risks with particular respect to sickness and length of life. We noted in chapter 2 that genetic insights already provide the means to determine individual probabilities for the occurrence of a small but growing group of serious illnesses which regularly involve high costs for care and medication and the likelihood of an early death. We also pointed to the substantial remaining uncertainties about the future potential of this science for medical risk assessments. Nevertheless, we deem it likely that additional genetic insights by 2010 will both widen and deepen the ability to determine individual risks, and so considerably increase the scope for implementing a system of actuarially based premium differentiation for discrete groups of insurance buyers. We conclude that the first precondition for the emergence of a profitable niche is already fulfilled, and is likely to be substantially strengthened in the course of the present decade.

The second precondition is that the restrictions on the use of genetic information in the field of personal insurance will not be globally applied. We deem complete global support for regulation in this field to be highly unlikely. Such global unanimity has not been achieved even for actions where the ethical, legal or practical arguments in favour of regulation have been much more clear-cut, for example to prevent the laundering of money earned in narcotics trade, or to thwart unambiguous tax fraud. As far as we know, there is no regulation that is in force throughout the world, even with regard to such crucial issues as basic human rights, or the production and storage of chemical and biological weapons. On this basis we consider it highly probable that some governments will choose to allow the use of genetic insights for determining personal insurance premiums, on the basis, for instance, that such practice assures a high degree of actuarial justice (pay the costs of the actual risk, neither more nor less), or because they deem it more important to nurture an efficient insurance sector than to promote equality in insurance premiums for individuals who represent different insurance risks. A further reason for refraining from participation in an international regulation effort in this field is that such a decision would undoubtedly attract big insurance companies to locate more of their business in the country in question.

We also deem it highly improbable that the insurance industry would voluntarily refrain from using genetic insights when such practice is legal in some countries, especially if the practice is known to strengthen competitiveness. Examples from other markets support our view. International insurance companies in tax havens with rigorous banking secrecy, for example Jersey or Switzerland, that handle pension capital for their foreign clients, obviously conduct their business within the realms of local legislation. At the same time they energetically market their products internationally even where it is quite evident that their clients commit offences against their home countries' fiscal rules by not declaring assets and returns at home. It is hard to believe that the insurers would act differently with regard to the legality and usage of genetic information.

With a continued deepening of global economic integration, we think it probable that the application of legislation extraterritorially, for instance in the form of the explicit prohibition of the purchase of foreign insurance that is not subject to regulation related to the use of genetic insights, will become increasingly rare. The issue of genetic insights application in insurance is simply not sufficient to give rise to far-reaching extraterritorial claims. In the absence of such extraterritorial application, individuals will be free to circumvent existing national rules by buying insurance elsewhere. Governments in countries where such regulation prevails can nevertheless deter international trade without outright prohibition. For instance, the marketing of foreign insurance products could be disallowed, or else the government could declare the insurance contracts void. Such deterrence would be easy to circumvent. The Internet can be used as a powerful marketing channel, while contractual disputes could be resolved in the country where the insurance was bought. The situation will then be akin to that of the British betting industry, but differ from that of German savings being moved to Luxembourg for the purpose of escaping German tax, in that the former merely evades national legislation without breaking any laws, while the latter involves a German criminal offence.

For all these reasons, it is highly probable that legislation in some countries will allow the use of genetic information for the purpose of insurance.

It is equally probable that insurance companies operating in such countries will make use of genetic information. Personal insurance with premiums that have been differentiated with the help of genetic insights will therefore be available in the international market. Those who live in countries subject to restrictive regulation in this field will in all probability not commit any specific legal offence if they buy such insurance products. The absence of extraterritorial restrictions in this context is not a precondition for the emergence of an international market, but it will undoubtedly increase the demand for personal insurance from countries where genetic technology has been used in determining premium levels.

5.3.2 A dynamic model[2]

The following calculations are hypothetical. They have to be, since we have currently no experience of the processes to be described. The purpose is primarily to give an idea of likely orders of magnitude, and of the dynamic processes that will promote international trade with insurance where the premiums have been differentiated with the help of genetics.

We focus for our example on the European Union at the turn of the century, comprising fifteen countries with a total population of 375 million, and with a labour force of 171 million (OECD, 2001, p. 22). We assume that social security transfers are financed solely by the labour force. In 1999, public expenditure for social insurance corresponded to 16.8 per cent of the area's GDP, US$1,430 billion in total (OECD, 2001, pp. 17, 67), or $8,400 per individual. Since the reforms towards the individualisation of social insurance have probably already reduced the public burden in some measure (as noted in chapter 4, the public cost for social insurance in the EU culminated in 1993 at a level corresponding to 18.3 per cent of GDP), it is clear that the total cost for the insurance protection under review must be higher than the numbers that we are using.

We now make two hypothetical assumptions on which our calculations are based. First, we take it that one third of the total social insurance cost will be individualised or outright privatised, implying freedom for the individuals to handle this part of their insurance protection as they deem fit. Our assumption posits that the state will continue to guarantee a base protection to the entire population, including those who do not contribute to the financing of the system, for instance because they never enter the labour market.

Our second assumption is based on the bold scenario (see chapter 2) regarding the prospects for genetic science to predict risks for illness and

---

[2] The analyses in Radetzki, 2001, have inspired the following presentation.

length of life. Thus, we take it that at the time when the transformation of social insurance posited above has been implemented, genetics will make it possible to divide the collective entity of the social insurance clients into two equal parts, and to assess that the half with low-risk genes will carry costs 25 per cent below the average for the entire group.

We underline that both assumptions are hypothetical, and that the purpose is not to predict what will occur in the future, but merely to create a basis for the ensuing calculations. In particular, the concept of 'bold' to characterise the scenario under review, could be seen as a misnomer. It is bold in the sense it suggests that genetics will be able to say something about the risks represented by all individuals in the population. But it is exceedingly prudent in positing that only two groups will be identified, and that the deviation between them in terms of cost of risk will be no more than 25 per cent, up or down, from the average. Later in the present section we present a set of alternative assumptions and starting points, still based on the bold scenario, and calculate their outcomes.

After the indicated social insurance reforms have been completed, the insured individuals can be expected to obtain proposals from insurance companies located offshore, to undertake genetic tests, and to sign insurance contracts at a cost that is 25 per cent below what they have to pay at home, where the use of genetic test results for the purpose of insurance is prohibited, all of course subject to a test result that indicates low-risk genes. Since the average cost at home of the individualised part of social insurance amounts to $2,800 (one third of $8,400), while the offshore premium will be $2,100, the potential annual saving to the individual will amount to $700, a sum sufficiently significant to warrant some effort on his part.

It is easy to show that once the move offshore has begun, it will lead to a gradually accentuated adverse selection among those who remain with the home-based insurance arrangements. Hence the tendency will be to increase the disadvantage for those who decide against proposals to undergo genetic testing, or who are never offered the lower premium in consequence of the test result. Say that a sufficient number of the insured agrees to undergo a test, and that 10 per cent of the entire collective is offered and accepts the lower-cost offshore alternative. The consequence of the removal of this low-risk group will be an increase of the average cost for the remaining 90 per cent of the insurance collective, from $2,800 to $2,900, all on the assumptions made above. The incentive to undertake a test to ascertain low-risk genes and lower insurance premiums for those who have not yet done so will be strengthened, since the gain increases from $700 to $800 a year.

As the move offshore continues, it is arguable that after some time four out of five persons with low-risk genes will have chosen to replace the insurance without genetic information by the cheaper arrangement on offer after 'positive' genetic testing. High-risk genes will now dominate the collective that has remained at home. The average cost for this collective (60 per cent of the original total) works out at $3,300, and the benefit of moving offshore for the remaining individuals with low-risk genes rises to $1,200 per year. The average cost for those remaining at home increases further, to $3,500, when the entire low-risk gene group has moved away. This vicious evolution towards increasing adverse selection in countries where the use of genetic information is prohibited, will be speeded up if insurance companies are forced to accept 'foreigners' with high-risk genes as clients.

The purpose of this somewhat simplistic calculation is to indicate the orders of magnitude and the dynamics of a process that can be slow to begin with, but that will accelerate as the advantage of the offshore offers increases. However, a number of qualifications must be introduced.

Genetic tests and the subsequent differentiation of insurance premiums will carry a cost that must ultimately be covered by the insured. The net gain will consequently be somewhat smaller than the numbers we have quoted. At the same time we argue that technical progress will in all probability reduce the cost of testing to a trivial level where the expenditure does not constitute a significant deterrent (see chapter 2).

Three types of insurance are the focus of our attention. The results from genetic tests can be expected to point in opposite directions for health and premature death insurance on the one hand, and insurance to secure a pension during old age on the other. A genetic make-up that indicates a low risk of ill health and premature death, should reasonably also indicate the high probability of a long life and extended pension payments. Hence the benefit of revealing low-risk genes will normally be limited to the first two types of insurance, while tests that show high-risk genes will typically reduce the premiums for a retirement pension. An individual with low-risk genes will therefore tend to procure his health and life insurance policies offshore, while buying his pension scheme from domestic insurers who have no access to genetic information. Since lower premiums will normally be offered on only one or two of the three insurance types, the financial incentives to move offshore will be correspondingly weaker.

The assumption that one third, neither more nor less, of the total social insurance cost will be individualised and privatised, is of course arbitrary. As shown in chapter 4, the ongoing reforms of social insurance still have a long way to go, while governments continue to exhibit a marked reluctance to raise the insured levels in line with rising incomes. On this evidence, we argue that the assumed share to be lifted off the collective and obligatory system is a feasible, even probable, reflection of the state of prevailing conditions at the end of the present decade.

The individualised part of social insurance for high income groups will involve larger amounts, and consequently higher premiums than the average for the entire collective of socially insured. The high income earners will consequently have stronger pecuniary incentives to undergo genetic tests for a chance of lower offshore premiums. This group can therefore be expected to constitute a vanguard that advances the beginning of the exit process. For similar reasons, the same group is already a vanguard in the case of cross-border tax avoidance.

Our assumption that genetic testing will be able to identify half the population with low-risk genes, and that the size of the risk difference between the two population groups will remain static, is of course quite crude. Genetic science is in the process of very rapid and dynamic development and in all probability it will gradually become possible to use genetic testing for a finer classification into a number of risk groups. The identifiable range of insurance risk can be expected to widen over time, as the technology is refined. Once the risk profiles have been identified, it will be possible to offer insurance to each group at premium levels that correspond to their respective risks. Two implications follow from these more detailed projections of what genetic science will offer in the future.

The first implication is that the group that represents the smallest risk will have particularly strong incentives to go offshore, for it will be offered insurance at particularly low prices. Like the high income earners, this group can be expected to act as a vanguard that speeds up the process of change.

Second, the possibility of identifying many risk groups implies that the movement offshore will not end once half the collective has exited, as was indicated in the above example. The average cost within the national system will continue to rise with the exit of each consecutive group, so that incentives to move are created even for the higher risk groups. In the extreme case, only the highest risk group will remain in the domestic insurance system.

It is of course possible to make hypothetical assumptions about the future potential of genetic science in the field of risk assessment, yielding conclusions that the gains from exiting will remain small, and that therefore adverse selection will never emerge as a serious problem for the domestic insurance system. With such conclusions, the motivation for writing the present book would collapse. Alternative assumptions, which appear much more likely given the current state of the art and the progress of genetic science, point in the same direction as the bold scenario whose likely consequences were described above. Our cautious scenario, briefly described below, does not venture much beyond what is already achievable by genetic science in the field of risk assessments.

Consider, then, the implications of the alternative assumption that genetic insights make it possible to identify a group representing 3 per cent of the population, afflicted by serious genetic disorders. This feat is not far removed from what is already realisable. Assume further that the insurance costs for the individuals in this group are assessed at ten times the average for the entire collective of insured. Again, the number we posit is not extreme, in the light of current realities in prosperous economies. It follows from these assumptions that the 97 per cent of the collective representing the low risks will impose costs on the insurer which are 28 per cent below the average for the entire group. This 97 per cent will then have even stronger economic incentives to exit the system than the half with low-risk genes in the example discussed above, based on the bold scenario. In this light, the bold scenario may not be very bold at all, and the ultimate consequences of the present case turn out to be much more dramatic. The exit process will not end when half the insured collective has moved out. On the contrary, the disintegration of the domestic system will accelerate, since the incentives to move will increase continuously as the share of the low risks that remain at home declines. In the end, only 3 per cent of the original collective will remain, and the insurance premiums will be ten times as high as they were to begin with.

The future potential of genetics to determine insurance risks is currently unclear. The calculations worked out in our examples may not reflect what will happen in the future. But they clearly show that within a broad range of assumptions about the future possibilities offered by genetic science in this field, a stream of exits of the lower risks, and the ensuing adverse selection, cannot be precluded, and, when it occurs, can cause serious problems to the domestic insurance system.

5.4   The ultimate consequence of trade

Our analyses lead to a compelling conclusion. The prohibition of the use of genetic insights for determining insurance risks and setting premiums in personal insurance is neither sustainable nor meaningful in the longer run, in a world where profit maximising firms supply such insurance products on a global market, and where some offshore actors are not subject to this regulation. The insurance firms that operate at home will clearly be damaged by the restrictive regulation, while at the same time the initial advantage of the regulation for those with high-risk genes will be gradually depleted and will ultimately disappear completely.

Access to genetic information provides an indubitable competitive advantage to insurance firms. Insurers that can avail themselves of such information will take market shares from the ones that cannot. The market of the latter enterprise group will gradually shrink, and ultimately comprise only the groups that represent the highest risks.

Where the ownership of the insurance enterprises is divided between the disadvantaged firms at home and those located offshore, one can expect the former to lobby politically for rules that assure neutral competitive conditions. A variety of measures to achieve such neutrality is conceivable. One method could be to subsidise the regulated firms, but then it would appear to be more rational to abolish the regulation, and to subsidise the premium payments for the disadvantaged individuals who represent genetically high risks (see chapter 8).

Another method could be to replace existing total regulation systems with partial regulation, prohibiting the requirement for new tests, but mandating the client to inform the insurance firm about the genetic tests that already exist. Theoretically, this could restore neutrality in competition between the enterprises located at home and those offshore, provided that the home firms are immediately informed about the outcome of tests undertaken on the initiative of the offshore firms, for then all the insurers would be able to offer actuarial premiums based on the test results. In practice, however, it is far from certain that an unconditional requirement on the individual to reveal the results of existing genetic tests would restore competitive neutrality. In an effort to maintain their competitive edge, the offshore firms that have taken the initiative to test could simply provide their potential clients with a premium offer, without revealing the full test results.

The insurers' lobbying against the restriction on the use of genetic information is likely to be much weaker where the market is dominated by globally active firms with subsidiaries both within and outside the regulation's reach. The global business of such firms should not be much affected by the regulation, even though the restrictions will result in an artificial and possibly inconvenient shift of much of the activity to offshore locations.

The main purpose of the prohibition against the use of genetic insights when personal insurance policies are formulated and sold is to promote a kind of justice. No one should have to pay more for his insurance to protect against sickness, invalidity and premature death, or to maintain income during old age, just because he has been endowed with genes that represent a higher insurance risk. But as we have demonstrated in the preceding section, such prohibition will be hard to sustain in a globally integrated economy where personal insurance is offered and bought in an international market.

We have also pointed to the continuously increasing adverse selection of the domestic insurance company's clients, as larger numbers of groups with genes that represent low insurance risks are offered and accept insurance with lower premiums offshore. The consequence will be that the firms remaining at home will have to raise their premiums in order to cover the higher risks represented by the clients who do not move. If the process continues to its end, the result will be that all the groups identifiable with the help of genetics, except that representing the highest risk, will have found advantage in moving offshore and paying premiums that have been differentiated on the basis of each group's risk profile.

It is possible, even probable, that this development will result in a total collapse in the supply of the domestic personal insurance market, and that those who have relied on it will thus lose their insurance protection altogether.

But things will not be much better if insurance companies subject to the restrictive regulation continue to offer policies to the highest risk group that has not had reason to move. The high premiums that have to be paid by this group must be actuarial and not different from the premiums offered on the basis of genetic testing, for otherwise the commercial survival of the system will be threatened. The outcome for all risk groups will turn out to be exactly the same as it would have been if the prohibition against the use of genetic insights had never been set in force. This implies a complete eradication of the remaining, ethically based motive for the regulation of genetic insights in the determination of personal insurance premiums.

Based on the above analyses and discussions, we argue that the regulation of genetic insights for the purpose of insurance is not sustainable. It will be brought to an end once it is realised that it does not serve its ethical goals. The problems of equity that are bound to arise in consequence will have to be handled by the authorities, and we discuss in chapter 8 some possible policy solutions. But it is essential at this stage of our discourse to point to a set of important side benefits that will arise as the regulation is repealed. Only then will it be possible fully to combine the potential offered by genetics with the insurers' interests, to improve the life of the insured with higher genetic risk through the development of preventive measures and prophylactic treatment, and at the same time to reduce the cost to the insurers of carrying that risk.

6 Prohibitions against discrimination in the private sphere: does legislation build on a consistent foundation?

6.1 Introduction

Our general hypothesis is that existing restrictions on the access of insurance companies to genetic information will hardly prove possible to sustain in their entirety in the long term. The decisive reason why this is so is that, as became clear in chapter 5, these regulations will be unable to fulfil their intended purpose. At first sight it might seem as if this in itself would suffice to verify the hypothesis we have advanced. However, a closer examination indicates that some regulations remain in force even though they fail to fulfil their intended purposes. One major reason for this may be that the regulations are part of a larger system building on a consistent foundation and there is a general idea that everything possible should be done to maintain the unified character of this regulatory system.

As an example of a system of regulations constructed on a fairly consistent basis, we may cite the legislation in many countries covering income tax. Although this legislation is unable to satisfy the underlying fiscal intention in certain respects (for example, where mutual favours are concerned), the regulations remain unchanged out of regard for the consistency of the body of regulations as a whole. In contrast, we could cite the regulatory framework for the taxation of wealth, where the general liability to pay taxes is widely curtailed by exemptions motivated by a variety of reasons.

For our general hypothesis – that existing restrictions on the access of insurance companies to genetic information are unlikely to be maintained – to be considered verified with any degree of certainty, it is therefore not enough that the regulations cannot fulfil their purpose. Over and above this, it is necessary that the restrictions we have discussed cannot be fitted into a system of regulations that rests on a consistent foundation. This chapter aims to investigate whether this second condition is also met.

From a practical perspective, it is probably fair to say that the most striking effect of the regulations restricting the access of insurance companies to genetic information is to prevent the companies exercising discrimination[1] on genetic grounds. From a legal point of view, these restrictions thus belong in the first instance to the body of regulations prohibiting various types of discrimination.[2] We therefore investigate whether this latter body of regulations has a consistent and differentiating foundation. If it should be the case that the legislation on discrimination builds on a consistent and differentiating foundation, the question will arise whether the regulations limiting the access of insurance companies to genetic information can be fitted into this body of regulations. As will, however, become clear (section 6.3.4), it has proved impossible to identify any consistent and differentiating criteria behind the legislation on discrimination and as a result we have found it unnecessary to investigate the latter question.

A few introductory remarks addressing such issues as the distinction between discrimination in the public and private spheres (sections 6.2 and 6.3.1) will be followed by a brief account of the principle of freedom of contract (section 6.3.2) and of a number of internationally relevant prohibitions against discrimination that are applied along with the ban on genetic discrimination in connection with insurance (section 6.3.3). In section 6.3.4 we analyse the reasons for these prohibitions. Here, the point of departure consists of the characteristics on the basis of which discrimination is not permitted. For what reason has discrimination on the basis of these particular characteristics – but not others – been prohibited? We attempt to discover some common denominator for these characteristics, something that justifies the prevailing prohibition against discrimination, some feature that other characteristics lack, with the result that discrimination based on these other characteristics has not been forbidden. Since it has not proved possible to identify such common and differentiating features, we conclude that the legislation on discrimination does not rest on a consistent foundation. In section 6.4 we discuss the consequences of this conclusion, focusing in particular on the access of insurance companies to genetic information.

---

[1] The concept of discrimination is used here in its most objective sense, according to which it covers any situation in which two cases are treated in different ways. Support for an objective definition of this kind may be found, for example, in the *Oxford English Dictionary* (1989). More evaluative positions, such as whether the special treatment is of a positive or negative nature, are thus irrelevant to the question as to whether discrimination can be said to exist. It does, however, happen that the meaning of the term is made to depend on evaluative elements of this kind (for example in *Collins English Dictionary* (1998)).

[2] Naturally, the existing limitations on the access of insurance companies to genetic information also have certain links with other systems of regulation. This might be an argument for extending the scope of the investigation in the present chapter to include these regulations too. In our opinion, though, the link is not sufficiently strong to justify an investigation of such breadth.

6.2   Discrimination in the public sphere

It is important to distinguish between discrimination in (i) the public and (ii) the private sphere. In the public sphere, like cases must be treated alike. This follows from a general principle that applies in all the countries included in our study.[3] By and large, it is the existing legal regulations that determine which cases are to be considered to be alike. Hence, an essential condition for discrimination in the public sphere is that it has the support of the law. For example, the right to vote in many countries is restricted to persons over the age of eighteen.

6.3   Discrimination in the private sphere

6.3.1   Introduction

However, the genetic discrimination on the part of insurance companies that the regulations at issue here are intended to prevent occurs not in the public but in the private sphere. Discrimination in the public sphere will therefore not be discussed further in this connection and in the following sections the concept of discrimination will refer solely to discrimination in the private sphere.

6.3.2   Freedom of contract as the point of departure

The states that are included in our study are all characterised by a market-oriented economic system. One of the fundamental elements of a market economy is freedom of contract. The concept of freedom of contract is in fact an umbrella term for three different but connected freedoms, namely, the freedom of the individual to enter into contracts or to refrain from doing so, the freedom to choose the party with whom they enter into a contract and the freedom to determine the contents of the contract.[4] It is obvious that these freedoms encompass a right to discriminate in the context of activities in the private sphere (cf. Schiek, 1999, p. 78). Such discrimination, moreover, occurs widely. A few everyday examples are special reduced charges for children, young people, pensioners and students in various connections, the specially reduced 'girl's rate' for taxi trips at night in some cities, and age limits at bars and night clubs in

---

[3] Fundamental support for this principle may be found in Article 27 of the International Covenant on Civil and Political Rights, adopted by the United Nations in 1966.

[4] For a general account of freedom of contract and its significance in a historical perspective, see Atiyah, 1979 and 1989.

some countries, which sometimes vary according to gender (for further examples see Banton, 1994, p. 2).

The freedom of contract, however, is not without restrictions. Mandatory contract regulations (regulations imposing an obligation to enter into a contract) are unusual but by no means unknown (for a detailed account see Nybergh, 1997). Something that occurs considerably more commonly are binding rules setting forth different minimum requirements relating to the contents of a contract.[5] Though these regulations obviously limit opportunities to discriminate, the effect is marginal: once the requirements of the binding regulations are satisfied, there is nothing to prevent special treatment.

6.3.3   Prohibitions against discrimination

Along with the limitations already mentioned, however, freedom of contract is curtailed by a number of explicit prohibitions against discrimination (Schiek, 1999, p. 78; cf. Atiyah, 1995, p. 106). Some examples of prohibitions of this kind that have international effect and are hence relevant to most of the countries included in our study are presented in the following sections. This account, though, is confined to some of the major legal instruments adopted by the United Nations (section 6.3.3.1) and the European Community (EC) (section 6.3.3.2).[6]

6.3.3.1 United Nations regulations   Under the 1965 International Convention on the Abolition of All Forms of Racial Discrimination, states parties to the convention undertake to guarantee every individual, without distinction on grounds of race, colour or national or ethnic origin, equality before the law, particularly with respect to the right of access on equal terms to any place and service intended for use by the general public, such as means of transport, hotels, restaurants, cafés, theatres and parks (Article 5 (f)).

6.3.3.2 EC law   Article 12 of the Treaty Establishing the European Community (the EC Treaty) rules that all discrimination on grounds of nationality[7] shall be prohibited. This prohibition applies not just to open (direct) discrimination but also to discrimination that is hidden (indirect),

---

[5] These minimum requirements apply to a large number of different circumstances, for example, the right to complain about faults in purchased goods.

[6] We make no claim to exhaustive treatment even with respect to legal instruments issued by these two organisations.

[7] The concept of nationality is used as a synonym for the concept of citizenship in this connection.

in the sense that while criteria other than nationality are made the apparent basis for special treatment, the result is the same as if discrimination occurred directly for reasons of nationality. Examples include unjustified language and residence requirements (Bernitz and Kjellgren, 1999, p. 103). This general prohibition against discrimination on the basis of nationality is defined in greater detail by a number of more precisely formulated prohibitions against discrimination in particular areas. Most of these refer primarily to discrimination in the public sphere, for example, in connection with the establishment of enterprises and the design of the tax system. With regard to discrimination in the private sphere, we may note in particular Article 39(2) of the EC Treaty, which states that all discrimination against workers from the member states based on nationality shall be abolished where employment, remuneration and other working and employment conditions are concerned.

Article 141 of the EC Treaty expresses the principle of equal pay for women and men for equal work or work of equal value. Accordingly, Council Directive 76/207/EC aims at implementing the principle of equal treatment for women and men as regards access to employment (including promotion), vocational training, working conditions and, subject to specially defined conditions, social security (Article 1). In these areas Article 2 of the Directive states that there shall be no discrimination whatsoever on grounds of gender either directly or indirectly. The provision does not, however, extend to so-called preferential treatment for the purposes of guaranteeing equality between women and men.

The two EC Treaty prohibitions against discrimination in the private sphere that have been discussed so far are supplemented by Article 13, which authorises the Council to take appropriate action to combat discrimination on grounds of sex, race, ethnic origin, religion or belief, disability, age or sexual orientation. Thus the provisions provide no direct foundation for requirements of equal treatment. On the other hand, the option is given of introducing regulations conferring the right to equal treatment by means of secondary legislation (Bergström, 1997, p. 312). At any event, pursuant to Article 13 – which was not adopted until 1997 as part of the Treaty of Amsterdam – two different directives entailing prohibitions against discrimination in the private sphere have come into being.

Council Directive 2000/43/EC prohibits all forms of direct and indirect discrimination on grounds of racial or ethnic origin (Article 2). According to Article 3, the areas that come within the scope of this prohibition against discrimination include working life, self-employment, vocational training including practical work experience, membership of and involvement in an organisation of workers or employers, health and medical care, social advantages, education, and access to and supply of goods and services.

Council Directive 2000/78/EC prohibits direct and indirect discrimination on grounds of religion or belief, disability, age or sexual orientation (Article 2). As specified by Articles 1 and 3, however, this prohibition is limited to working life, self-employment, vocational training including practical work experience, and membership of and involvement in an organisation of workers or employers.[8]

Finally, in this connection, we shall mention Council Directives 97/81/EC and 99/70/EC, the purpose of which is to implement the framework agreements on part-time and fixed-term work respectively that have been concluded between the social partners at European level[9] as part of EC law. The material provisions of these directives are given in the agreements mentioned, to which the directives refer. Clause 4 of each agreement directs that conditions of employment for part-time and fixed-term workers respectively shall be no less favourable than the conditions affecting comparable full-time or permanent workers simply because the former hold part-time or fixed-term contracts, unless this can be justified on objective grounds.

6.3.3.3 Conclusions   In the countries included in our study, the principle of freedom of contract prevails, and as a result the first assumption has to be that discrimination in the private sector must be considered to be permissible. However, the freedom of contract is not unrestricted. Alongside binding regulations of a general character relating to mandatory contracts and the contents of contracts, various legal instruments issued by the UN, EC and other bodies identify a number of grounds on which discrimination in the private sector is not regarded as acceptable. Among the unacceptable grounds for discrimination we may note race, colour, national or ethnic origin, nationality, gender, religion/belief, physical function, age and sexual orientation, as well as number of working hours and security of employment contract. Only a few of these prohibitions against discrimination, however, enjoy general application, namely those that target race, colour, national or ethnic origin and nationality. Others, in contrast – those that refer to discrimination based on religion/belief, gender,

---

[8] In what follows these sectors will be summed up in the term 'working life and associated areas'.

[9] Framework agreements for part-time work and fixed-term work respectively, concluded on 6 June 1997 and 18 March 1999 respectively between the Union of Industrial and Employers' Confederations of Europe (UNICE), the European Trade Union Confederation (ETUC) and the European Centre of Enterprises with Public Participation and of Enterprises of General Economic Interest (CEEP).

physical function, age, sexual orientation and number of working hours and security of employment contracts – are only applicable in the context of working life and associated areas.

6.3.4   Reasons for prohibiting discrimination

The characteristics on the basis of which discrimination is not permitted under the legislation in force are rather disparate in nature. Why have these particular characteristics been selected and subjected to prohibitions, while discrimination based on other characteristics, such as health, civil status, capital assets or social competence, encounters no legal obstacle?

In the following sections we investigate whether the different prohibitions against discrimination are based on one or more consistent fundamental criteria. In section 6.3.4.1 we note that no such consistent fundamental criteria have been expressed in the preparatory proceedings leading up to the different regulations. Nor is it possible to identify any consistent features among the characteristics that are not permitted to serve as a basis for discrimination that differentiate these from other characteristics (section 6.3.4.2). The various prohibitions against discrimination thus appear to have come into existence independently of any overall strategy on the part of the legislator. Our conclusion is that the legislation in the area of discrimination is not based on a consistent foundation. Rather, the different prohibitions against discrimination appear to be the result of a selective implementation of the principle of the equal value of all people derived from natural law, with clear political overtones (sections 6.3.4.3–6.3.4.4).

6.3.4.1 Legislative proceedings   The prohibitions against discrimination issued by the *United Nations* belong to the extensive body of regulations relating to human rights, albeit peripherally so.[10] This body of regulations, which came into being largely as a reaction against the brutal excesses of the Second World War (Clayton and Tomlinson, 2000, p. 3; Fisher,

---

[10] According to a narrow definition human rights are such 'fundamental rights that every individual is considered to be able to claim vis-à-vis the collective' (Fisher, 2001, p. 13). UN anti-discrimination regulations target discrimination in both the private and public spheres. In so far as the regulations target discrimination in the private sector (which is our primary interest) they would therefore fall outside the framework of regulations relating to human rights in a narrow sense of the term. It is nevertheless clearly the case that the UN's anti-discrimination regulations have come into existence as part of the work on human rights and so belong to that body of regulations. Accordingly, the regulations at issue here are discussed in their entirety in the great majority of accounts of human rights (for example, Danelius, 1993, pp. 29 f.).

2001, p. 13), was prepared by extensive groundwork. Nevertheless, no substantial discussion, taking up fundamental principles, appears to have been devoted to the choice of characteristics on the basis of which discrimination is not permitted. Moreover, as far as is known, this topic has been discussed neither in connection with the implementation of the regulations in national law nor in the legal literature.

Since the 1960s human rights have played an increasingly important part in *EC law*, a trend that has accelerated in the last few years (von Bogdandy, 2000, p. 1307). One of several expressions of this influence is Article 13 of the Treaty of Amsterdam, on non-discrimination (cf. Lenaerts, 2000, p. 578). This provision represents the result of a compromise between, on the one hand, the view that EC law should be inspired by the body of regulations relating to human rights, and so contain a broad prohibition against discrimination, and on the other hand, the view that issues relating to discrimination should be addressed within the framework of the member states' national legal systems (cf. Flynn, 1999, pp. 1129 ff.).

The member states have not always seen eye to eye on the grounds for discrimination that the prohibitions in the Community's legal regulations ought to cover, and these differences have led to negotiations and compromises. Hence, negotiations between the EU countries on the grounds for discrimination that ought to be included in Article 13 of the Treaty of Amsterdam continued up to the eleventh hour. The scope of the provision was extended at a late stage from discrimination on the basis of religious belief to discrimination on the basis of religion or belief. Conversely, social origin, which was included in a number of different proposals with a view to protecting the Roma and other groups, was left out. A motion that disability and sexual orientation should also be eliminated as grounds for discrimination failed, on the other hand, to win support (Flynn, 1999, pp. 1131 f.). However, no substantial discussion occurred regarding the reasons behind the views in question. Nevertheless, a few documents do indicate that the frequent occurrence of discrimination based on certain characteristics played a significant role.[11] This point has also been underlined in connection with the implementation of the regulations in national law.[12] Otherwise, though, the choice of characteristics on the

[11] See the proposed Directives COM/99/0565 (especially section II) and COM/99/0566 (especially section 2), which, when adopted, received the designations 2000/78/EC and 2000/43/EC respectively.

[12] See Prop 1997/98:177 (concerning new Swedish legislation on measures against discrimination in working life), p. 14 (under the heading 'General considerations'): 'The situation on the labour market in recent years, with high unemployment and falling

basis of which discrimination is not allowed has been discussed neither in this connection nor in the legal literature. It must be observed, however, that what we have just said is subject to one important exception. The prohibition against discrimination on the basis of nationality has been justified in detail with reference to the Community's endeavour to establish a common internal market based on an open market economy and free competition (Bernitz and Kjellgren, 1999, p. 103).

6.3.4.2 Does anti-discrimination legislation build on a consistent and differentiating foundation? There are explicit prohibitions preventing discrimination on the basis of race, colour, ethnic/national origin, nationality, gender, religion/belief, physical function, age, sexual orientation and number of working hours/security of employment contract. There is nothing to prevent discrimination on other grounds, including health, civil status, capital assets and social competence. On top of this, the prohibitions against discrimination on grounds of gender, religion/belief, physical function, age, sexual orientation and number of working hours/security of employment contract apply only to working life and associated areas. Hence, in other connections discrimination on these grounds is permitted. As has become clear, the selective process that obviously lies behind the existing legislation on discrimination has not been openly discussed during the legislative proceedings. Yet this does not exclude the possibility that the selection is nevertheless based on one or more consistent though unspoken criteria. This being so, it is important to attempt to clarify by more detailed analysis, first, whether the characteristics that constitute grounds for anti-discrimination regulations exhibit any shared features that motivate their selection, and, second, whether these features differentiate the characteristics mentioned from characteristics that are acceptable grounds for discrimination.

Shared features. One feature that all the characteristics on the basis of which discrimination is not allowed share is that on the basis of that characteristic, a not inconsiderable amount of discrimination does actually occur or can be expected to occur in the foreseeable future.[13] Moreover, the existence of all the characteristics in question can be established on an

economic activity rates, has hit individuals from foreign backgrounds and individuals belonging to one or other of Sweden's historical national minorities particularly hard. For certain groups from foreign backgrounds the unemployment figures are well nigh catastrophic . . . In the second half of 1997 just over half of non-Nordic citizens were outside the labour market and unemployment in this population had become six times as high as in 1990.'

[13] This is hinted at already in the preparatory groundwork for some anti-discrimination regulations. See further section 6.3.4.1.

objective basis. Evidently, the legislator is disinclined to prohibit discrimination on the basis of characteristics whose existence can only be established by an act of valuation. This approach appears to be well motivated. A regulation prohibiting discrimination against, for example, unpleasant people would be extremely problematic to put into practice.

Further, it appears to be commonly held that anti-discrimination regulations are only possible if discrimination is based on a fundamental characteristic that the individual is compelled to live with whether he or she wants to or not.[14] A prohibition against discrimination therefore requires that three different conditions be met. It must be a matter of (i) a fundamental characteristic, (ii) of a permanent nature that (iii) the individual can do nothing to change.[15] Table 6.1 shows that most of the anti-discrimination regulations address characteristics that meet these criteria. However, it is clear that a prohibition against discrimination does not necessarily require that all three criteria be satisfied. Alongside the circumstances that have already been mentioned, there may be reason to examine the economic effects of exercising or being subject to discrimination on the basis of characteristics specified in table 6.1.

For a person who is subjected to discrimination, it probably matters little from an economic point of view whether this discrimination is based on ethnic origin, gender, health or some other factor. Consequently it hardly seems likely that the economic effects of being subjected to discrimination or not have had any influence on the choice of characteristics on which prohibitions against discrimination are based. For the victim, the economic effects of discrimination probably have more to do with the context in which discrimination occurs. The economic impact of being exposed to discrimination ought normally to be greater when discrimination occurs in working life than when it occurs in connection with the exercise of some spare-time activity.[16] Legislators appear to be especially inclined to issue regulations prohibiting discrimination when the economic consequences threaten to be particularly serious. This is clearly

---

[14] The Swedish Ombudsman against Ethnic Discrimination, Anders Kandelin, has expressed this view in a private conversation.

[15] These criteria are obviously not exact. What is *fundamental* is a matter of evaluation. Whether a characteristic (such as a disability) is *permanent* or is *possible to change* may vary according to the circumstances in each particular case. What is *possible to change*, moreover, depends on the demands that can reasonably be made on the individual. The classification undertaken in table 6.1 is an attempt to reflect what may be considered to correspond to the prevailing opinion with respect to a normal case.

[16] With regard to the provision of goods and services, the economic effect apparently varies similarly according to the significance of the commodities concerned (cf. Sandberg, 1996, p. 85).

Table 6.1. *Characteristics that may not be made the basis for discrimination and some of their features*

Characteristic	Fundamental	Permanent	Impossible to change
Race	Yes	Yes	Yes
Colour	Yes	Yes	Yes[a]
Ethnic/national origin	Yes	Yes	Yes
Nationality	Yes	Yes	Yes[b]
Sex	Yes	Yes	Yes[c]
Religion/belief	Yes	Yes	Yes[d]
Physical function[e]	Yes	Yes	Yes
Age	Yes	No	Yes
Sexual orientation	Yes	Yes	Yes[f]
Working hours/contract security	No	Yes	No

[a] Technically speaking it is possible to change colour. Moreover, such cases do actually occur (for example the American singer Michael Jackson). Nevertheless, as this type of procedure is very uncommon, it seems reasonable to ignore this possibility.

[b] It has already been made clear that the concept of nationality is used here as a synonym of citizenship (section 6.3.3.2). There is of course some possibility of changing nationality. However, the chances of doing so are often so limited and so tied to various conditions that the individual can by no means be said to have control over his or her nationality.

[c] Technically speaking it is possible to change sex, and cases do occur. Nevertheless, as this type of procedure is very uncommon, it seems reasonable to ignore this possibility.

[d] On the surface it is of course possible for the individual to change his or her own religious or other beliefs. At a *deeper level*, though, this is surely hardly possible.

[e] By this we mean the existence or absence of a disability (handicap).

[f] On the surface it is of course possible for the individual to change his or her own sexual orientation. At a *deeper level*, though, this is surely hardly possible.

evident from the fact that most of the prohibitions against discrimination described in section 6.3.3 are applicable in working life and associated areas but not in other connections.

The economic results of discrimination or refraining from discrimination are probably also largely, if not solely, dependent on the circumstances in which discrimination occurs. Since most of the prohibitions against discrimination listed in table 6.1 are only applicable in working life and associated areas, the following account naturally focuses on the economic significance of being able to discriminate in this particular connection.

It is scarcely feasible to set out a generally applicable scale of the economic significance of discrimination based on different characteristics. The circumstances vary from case to case. On the other hand, it is possible to state whether the existence of a certain characteristic *as such* is capable of affecting a worker's ability to perform working tasks, or whether this characteristic only acquires such significance in combination with other people's attitudes.[17] In the first case, the characteristic has direct economic significance; in the second its economic significance is of an indirect nature.

Using this terminology we are able to establish that the economic significance of most of the characteristics on the basis of which discrimination may not occur is of an indirect nature. However, there is nothing to prevent discrimination on the basis of a feature that has direct economic significance coming under a prohibition at some time. This is clear from the existing prohibitions against discrimination in working life on grounds of disability.

Do the shared features have the power to give rise to differentiation? The different characteristics on the basis of which discrimination has been forbidden exhibit two common features. First, it is a matter of characteristics on the basis of which a more than inconsiderable amount of discrimination actually occurs or can be expected to occur in the foreseeable future. Second, what are involved are characteristics whose existence can be confirmed by objective criteria. That these are necessary conditions for the establishment of a prohibition against discrimination appears probable. Yet some characteristics exist that in spite of exhibiting these two features have not led to a prohibition against discrimination (a number of examples are given below). The two features are therefore by no means differentiating criteria.

Furthermore, we have established that the great majority of the characteristics that have led to prohibitions against discrimination meet all or at least two of the criteria given in table 6.1, namely, (i) fundamental, (ii) permanent and (iii) not possible to change. Over and above this, it has become clear that the economic significance of being able to exercise discrimination in working life on the basis of the features that have led to prohibitions against discrimination in most cases is merely of an indirect nature. However, exceptions do occur. Hence, these cannot be said to be necessary conditions for prohibitions against discrimination.

One apparently plausible interpretation of what has now been said might be that the probability of a prohibition against discrimination increases as an increasing number of the criteria discussed are met. However, this interpretation is open to question. As has become clear, characteristics do exist whose existence can be objectively established

---

[17] As an example of the latter we could cite a salesman whose ethnic origin combined with the intolerant attitude of the intended customers can be expected to affect the salesman's chances of selling his goods.

and on the basis of which discrimination does in fact occur, yet which have not occasioned any prohibition against discrimination. And this is true even when the characteristics in question exhibit some or most of the features mentioned in the previous paragraph. One such characteristic is health. In the light of existing prohibitions against discrimination in working life on the basis of physical function, it may be considered strange that discrimination on the basis of a person's state of health encounters no legal obstacle. To give further examples of characteristics on the basis of which discrimination is permitted, even though these characteristics exhibit various features that are typically indicative of prohibitions against discrimination, it is sufficient to recall the fact that many prohibitions against discrimination are only applicable in working life and associated areas. In other connections, therefore, discrimination on the basis of gender, religion/belief, physical function, age, sexual orientation and number of working hours/security of employment contract is completely legal.[18] All the indications are that the priority thus given to working life in drawing up discrimination legislation is due to legislators having considered it particularly important for the individual not to be subjected to discrimination in this particular sector of life. But working life is not unique in being important. Other sectors that have a significant role are the housing and insurance sectors. Yet in spite of this there is nothing in the internationally applicable regulation in the field of discrimination to prevent a private housing company discriminating against, say, Muslims. Moreover, the prioritisation of working life has not been implemented consistently. As has become evident, the prohibition against discrimination on the basis of ethnic origin, for example, is also applicable outside working life. The result – that the housing company is permitted to discriminate on the basis of religion but not on the basis of ethnic origin – clearly demonstrates the absence of a consistent and differentiating foundation to discrimination legislation.

Conclusions. The account given in this section has addressed the issue of what the characteristics of race, colour, ethnic/national origin, nationality, gender, religion/belief, physical function, age, sexual orientation and number of working hours/security of employment contract have in common to motivate existing anti-discrimination legislation and that other characteristics lack, with the result that they are not subject to anti-discrimination legislation. Even if most of the characteristics discussed have certain similarities, *it has not been possible to identify any completely*

---

[18] In some countries, however, the prohibitions against discrimination on the basis of religion/belief and sexual orientation have been extended to areas other than working life and associated areas.

consistent and differentiating features. Consequently, there are strong indications that existing anti-discrimination legislation lacks a consistent foundation.[19]

6.3.4.3 Do prohibitions against discrimination derive from natural law?

General remark on natural law. The fundamental idea of natural law (Strömholm, 1996, pp. 82 f.) is based on the assumption that there is in nature, that is independently of legislation and other human jurisdiction, an inherent set of principles and rules that together constitute a type of higher law. Essentially, the principles of natural law have binding force regardless of the substance of positive law. For the sake of order, however, it becomes the task of the legislator to implement natural law in the positive law. One of the main problems facing advocates of natural law is to find a convincing way of explaining the origin and existence of this higher system of law. Various explanatory models occur in this connection. One has a theological orientation, asserting that the higher order of natural law corresponds to the will of God. A second model is relative. According to this explanation, natural law consists of the minimum set of ethically necessary rules that need to underlie the actually implemented legal system of a society at a given stage of historical and cultural development.[20] Unlike other adherents of natural law, the advocates of relative natural law make no claim to have found an eternal, immutable and universally applicable system. Hence, relative natural law can vary over time and from place to place.

Even if the doctrine of natural law does not occupy a strong position in the legal systems of the Western world, it is by no means lacking in importance. Its claim to validity was raised, for example, during the trials of war criminals after the Second World War. The persecution laws applied by the Nazi regime were declared to be invalid with reference to morality and justice. Thus the war criminals were sentenced in accordance with rules that had no backing in the legal system that was in force when the acts were committed (Hellner, 1994, p. 23). Moreover, the body of regulations on human rights that emerged as one consequence of the war is

---

[19] Naturally, it is impossible to rule out completely the possibility that the characteristics on the basis of which discrimination is not permitted to occur do, in spite of everything, possess some shared and differentiating feature that we have missed. But the likelihood that this is so is probably limited, as the work done for this chapter has largely consisted of a search for a feature of this kind. Various features over and above those to which attention has explicitly been drawn were thus included in our investigation.

[20] In addition, there are at least two further variants of natural law, the rationalistic and the naturalistic.

commonly held to rest on a natural law foundation (Fisher, 2001, p. 13; Weissbrodt, 1988 p. 1).[21]

Natural law and the foundation of anti-discrimination regulations. Within natural law there is an overriding principle that all people are of equal value. In effect, this principle implies a right to equal treatment, that is a prohibition against discrimination. In positive law this principle has long been in force in the public sphere, where a general prohibition against discrimination applies (section 6.2). In the private sphere, on the other hand, the principle has merely held a subordinate place. Thus, unless otherwise specifically proscribed, discrimination is permitted (section 6.3).

The absence of any discussion of substance regarding the selection of characteristics on the basis of which discrimination is not permitted in the private sphere (section 6.3.4.1) undeniably awakens the impression that these regulations ultimately rest on the natural law principle that all people are of equal value. Discrimination on the grounds in question has obviously been regarded as unfair, with the result that the legislator, following natural law, has introduced prohibitions against discrimination into the material law. This impression is reinforced by the fact that the United Nations prohibitions against discrimination make up a part of the body of regulations relating to human rights, which rest on this principle and are thus coloured by natural law, while the various prohibitions against discrimination in European Community law evidently owe their genesis to the same spirit (section 6.3.4.1).

6.3.4.4 Conclusion: anti-discrimination legislation rests on a decidedly political foundation

By means of the prohibitions against discrimination in the private sphere, the natural law principle that all people are of equal value, along with the prohibitions against discrimination that follow from it – a principle that has traditionally only been applied in the public sphere – has been implemented in legislation relating to the private sphere. However, this implementation has not been carried out consistently. Prohibitions against discrimination in the private sphere are selective in nature. No reasons have been adduced as to why the principle of the equal value of all people shall be applied in certain cases but not in others (section 6.3.4.1). Nor do the different prohibitions against discrimination exhibit any consistent and differentiating ground on which existing special regulations can be justified (section 6.3.4.2). Anti-discrimination legislation is thus based on certain values being assigned superiority over others, without the reason for this being elucidated by analysis and debate. The

---

[21] Cf. Hellner, 2001, p. 130, who talks about the significance of natural law for international law, to which the body of regulations relating to human rights can be said to belong.

outcome is arbitrariness and obscurity (cf. Hellner, 1994, p. 24). Against this background, the extraordinary difficulty encountered by the EC countries in agreeing on which grounds for discrimination are to be made the object of a prohibition (section 6.3.4.1) may take on significance.

What governs the contents of legislation on discrimination thus appears to be what is on the political agenda at any particular time. It is significant that anti-discrimination legislation has been generated in recent times in favour of, for example, women and homosexuals, which are both groups that have successfully managed to organise themselves and win the support of public opinion for their own cause. The media clearly play a crucial role in this connection by their contribution to the political agenda.

In these circumstances, future legal developments in the area of discrimination are difficult to foresee. New prohibitions against discrimination will in all probability be produced as representatives of different special interests succeed in convincing decision-makers that their particular group is at risk. But it is uncertain which groups will win protection. Pregnant women, people on parental leave, substance abusers or some other group may come into question. At the same time, the absence of a consistent foundation for all prohibitions against discrimination means that the legislation in this area can be torn up without any need to take a position on fundamental legal issues. This being so, the security deriving from the legislation on discrimination in its present form has to be considered to be rather limited.

6.4   Concluding remarks

Our study shows that it is hardly possible to identify any generally applicable criteria governing the type of discrimination that is to be considered permissible or unacceptable. Our conclusion is therefore that the regulations that broadly prevent genetic discrimination in connection with insurance do not fit into a system of regulations that rests on a consistent foundation.[22]

Like other prohibitions against discrimination, the regulations relating to the right of insurance companies to make use of genetic information therefore appear to be rooted in a political will tending in a certain direction, not in any larger system of legal regulations on discrimination in the private sphere erected on a consistent foundation. Since the regulations

---

[22] Hence no need arises to investigate more specifically whether the prohibition against genetic discrimination in connection with insurance differs from the criteria that otherwise apply to anti-discrimination legislation (chapter 5, section 5.1). According to what we have established, it has been impossible to identify any such criteria.

that hinder genetic discrimination in connection with insurance have thus come into being without any legal considerations relating to matters of principle, they can probably be abolished without reference to any such considerations.

It is, incidentally, not so surprising that genetic technology has been specifically singled out for attention, with prohibitions against discrimination in connection with insurance as the result. There are many examples of people initially taking a negative attitude to the consequences of new technology. However, it often happens that such an attitude is a very temporary one. When the technology has become established and its potential benefits have become clear, attitudes commonly change. With the passing of time, only a few people react to phenomena that were previously felt by the great majority to be unacceptable. Instead the focus shifts to the positive effects of the technology concerned. One example of this process is heart transplants. The development of this technology was prevented early on by ethical arguments in many countries, including the United States, with the result that it initially moved to South Africa where there were no such obstacles. Once the technology had been established and attention drawn to its positive results, attitudes changed completely. In the twenty-first century, heart transplants are accepted throughout the Western world. The contraceptive pill presents a similar example. Early on, this product encountered stiff resistance even in non-Catholic circles. With the passage of time, the resistance has ebbed away.

Consequently, it is fully possible that in future genetic discrimination will not be felt to be any more problematic than the completely accepted discrimination that at present occurs on the basis of health. Moreover, the conclusion we reached in chapter 5 was that increased international trade in personal insurance will lead to the regulations preventing genetic discrimination in connection with insurance gradually losing their power. In view of this, in our opinion there is cause to review these regulations even now. In this chapter we have shown that such a review does not run into any fundamental obstacles from a legal point of view.

Part III

Ethical aspects

7 Ethical arguments for and against the right of insurance companies to genetic information

7.1 Introduction

The background to our discussion is the ability to determine the risk of onset of disease and premature death by presymptomatic and predictive genetic testing (chapter 2). The worries and hopes to which this has given rise are reflected in the ethical debate about genetics and insurance. The ethical question most commonly discussed in this particular context is the question of insurance companies' access to and use of genetic information.

This key issue can be subdivided into two questions. (i) Should insurance companies be allowed to demand that a previously untested person applying for insurance be tested? (ii) Should insurance companies have the right to information from tests that have already been conducted?[1] If the answer to the first question is yes, it will obviously be yes for the latter too. There is no point in insurance companies asking for a new test if they are not granted access to the information from it when the test is made. The reverse, however – the proposition that insurance companies should be allowed to ask for the results from past tests, but not to demand new ones – is a position that can be taken and has indeed been defended.[2]

There are two reasons for emphasising the distinction between these two kinds of regulation. First, this has been the primary distinction made in previous discussion of the regulation of insurance companies' access to genetic information. Second, and this explains the first reason, there are important differences between the two forms of regulation with regard to

---

[1] A distinction between access to and use of genetic information has been made (Mayer et al., 1999, p. 42). In this discussion the distinction will be ignored. It is taken for granted that the right to access genetic information implies a right to use that information to differentiate premiums and that a prohibition against access to genetic information also implies a prohibition against using it for premium differentiating purposes.

[2] For instance Sandberg, 1995, has defended this position, at least if the insured amount is above a certain specified amount. Below this amount companies should not have access to previous tests either.

autonomy, privacy and economic consequences, as will be evident in the following.

The position that insurance companies should be allowed both to ask for the results of previous tests and to demand that the individual undergo testing in order to be insured will in the following be called *absence of regulation*.[3] The position that insurance companies should be allowed to ask for the results of previous tests but not to demand new ones is called *partial regulation* (chapter 1). The position that insurance companies should be granted no access whatsoever to genetic information (at least not from genetic testing) is called *total regulation* (chapter 1). There are of course intermediate degrees between these notional types of regulation. In Sweden, for instance, access to results from previous tests is permitted only when the insured amount exceeds a pre-specified amount equivalent to about US$ 61,000 (see chapter 3, section 3.2.3).

The point of departure for this chapter is the hypothesis that insurance companies have an unrestricted right to ask for genetic information. That is, in the following discussion, absence of regulation is assumed. The question is, then, if such absence of regulation is ethically acceptable or if insurance companies' access to genetic information should be regulated and, if so, how. The purpose here is to provide an overview of the different ethical considerations that have been brought to bear in the discussion, and to evaluate these considerations.

An important insight of this chapter is that the question of insurance companies' access to genetic information must be answered against the background of how a particular society's institutions are designed and what role insurance companies play in this society. An important conclusion is that no individual should be left without access to goods that are vital to his welfare in an affluent society, simply because of his genes. Several basic ethical arguments support this conclusion.

Ethical concerns of many kinds have been raised in this context, suggesting that a classification of different ethical considerations is necessary. The most frequently recurring and important ethical reasons or arguments for and against insurance companies' access to genetic information will be categorised as follows: (i) arguments of consequences in terms of welfare; (ii) arguments of autonomy; (iii) arguments of privacy; and (iv) arguments of justice.

It is important to emphasise at this point that different ethical considerations can support different conclusions. Considerations of privacy, as

---

[3] 'Absence of regulation' is somewhat of a misnomer, since we presuppose that even under such conditions institutions exist which can sanction breaches of insurance contracts (such as omitting to follow the duty of disclosure, chapter 3, section 3.1).

will be demonstrated further on, seem to speak straightforwardly in favour of total regulation, while some considerations of consequence seem to favour partial regulation or even absence of regulation. It might seem, therefore, that in order to answer the question as to the sort of regulation there should be, one has to take a stand on the relative weight of these different ethical considerations. Appearances are deceptive, however. In the following, we will argue that in spite of their theoretical differences, several reasonable ethical theories seem to point in the same direction when it comes to more general conclusions. Furthermore, it is hardly possible to defend a full-blown ethical theory in this limited context. That would require far more than this inquiry can encompass. Nevertheless, we hope to show that we can learn something about ethical theory in general by applying different ethical theories to more concrete questions such as this. For instance, we will argue that this particular discussion shows that questions of privacy are secondary to or derived from other ethical concerns (at least in this context), and that some ideas of justice are dubious or altogether unacceptable (section 7.5.3). Apart from this, no stance will be taken regarding the relative weight of consequences of welfare versus justice, or justice versus autonomy, or consequences of welfare versus autonomy. Each of these ethical considerations is assumed to carry some moral weight.

The conclusions argued for in previous chapters are taken for granted in the following ethical discussion. Therefore, it is appropriate to present a brief summary of the most important conclusions before we go on. Regulation of insurance companies' access to genetic information has been implemented in several countries on ethical grounds. We have argued that the sustainability of regulation in this area is questionable for several reasons, the most important being that insurance companies under regulation will suffer from adverse selection (chapter 3, section 3.3.2). The possibility of buying insurance offshore will increase the severity of this problem (chapter 5, sections 5.2–5.3). There are, furthermore, no fundamental legal objections that can be brought to bear against abolishing regulation, since it is not a part of any consistent system of rules or laws (chapter 6, section 6.4).

If, for all these reasons, regulation breaks down, while the welfare state and its collectively funded social insurance system is being partially dismantled (chapter 4, section 4.4), the result will be an ethically unacceptable lack of insurance among genetically high-risk individuals. The initial establishment of regulation will therefore not serve the intended ethical goals.

In chapter 8, a policy to solve the problems caused by the breakdown of regulation will be presented. Before that, in this chapter, the ethical arguments for and against regulation of insurance companies' access to genetic information will be discussed.

7.2   Negative consequences

7.2.1   Consequentialism

Consequentialism, as defined here, is the position that the moral status of actions is determined solely by the value of their consequences in terms of welfare, compared with available alternatives. An action is right if, and only if, there is no other action the agent could have performed that would have resulted in more welfare (and/or less negative welfare). The same applies to societal institutions and laws: we should implement the institution or law that has the best possible consequences in terms of welfare, given the circumstances in which the institution or law is implemented. Welfare can be understood either as internal wellbeing (hedonism) or as preference satisfaction (preferentialism).[4] This doctrine is sometimes called utilitarianism.[5]

Consequentialism can thus be characterised as comprising two parts: one that defines what, ultimately, is of value (here we restrict ourselves to welfare) and one that says that value ought to be maximised and negative value (e.g. anxiety, pain and other forms of 'ill-faring') minimised. The welfare of an individual is influenced by a range of psychological, economic and other factors. According to consequentialism, all these factors are of relevance when the rightness or wrongness of an action or an institution is evaluated. To put it another way: an action can lead to the realisation of welfare (which has value in itself) or to something which in turn leads to the realisation of welfare (this, then, has instrumental value). Wellbeing, for instance, has value in itself, while physical exercise can lead to improved health, which may give the individual more and/or a stronger feeling of wellbeing (physical exercise then has instrumental value).

Much criticism can be brought to bear upon consequentialism in this form (Williams, 1973). As already mentioned, we basically ignore the question of the relative weight of welfare consequences compared with other ethical considerations. However, since it is hardly reasonable to maintain that the welfare of people has no weight when it comes to

---

[4] For a modern defence of classical consequentialism, see Tännsjö, 1998. The two most influential works on utilitarianism, which is embraced by consequentialism, are those of Bentham, 1789, and Mill, 1863.

[5] While consequentialism and utilitarianism are overlapping doctrines, for the sake of our argument the terms will here be held to be synonymous.

assessing the morality of actions, institutions or laws, the assumption that it carries some moral weight will be made.

In this context, however, a more disturbing problem associated with consequentialism comes to the fore. In the debate, attention has focused on a few of the probably many consequences of different forms of regulation, and the discussion has centred heavily on the negative consequences. Why this selection? Is it not possible that there are other important consequences to consider – consequences about which it is hard to say anything for sure? Can consequentialism ever be action-guiding, considering the many consequences of different realised and non-realised optional regulations? More generally, in the light of the obvious gaps in our knowledge, how can we compare the welfare of different persons to make a reasonable judgement when choosing between regulations on the basis of consequentialist premises?

We will sidestep rather than tackle all of these obvious problems, by concentrating on the most widely discussed welfare consequences of different forms of regulation. These are so salient that a consequentialist cannot ignore them. Further, the fact that we cannot give an exhaustive account should not prevent us from saying something, especially given the obvious importance to people's welfare that the discussed consequences could have. Moreover, the problem of having enough knowledge to make the ethical theory action-guiding is not unique to consequentialism (section 7.3.3).

The point of departure for the reasoning that follows is, then, absence of regulation. The question for consequentialism will thus be: what are the likely consequences if there is no regulation of insurance companies' access to genetic information? One obvious probable negative consequence in terms of welfare is that people of sufficiently high risk will become uninsured. Presymptomatic and predictive genetic testing makes it possible to differentiate individuals at high risk of developing conditions that will result in illness or death. Insurance companies will want to charge these people higher premiums in order to compensate for the greater risk of paying compensation, or maybe deny them insurance altogether if the risk is considered too great. Whether these people are denied insurance altogether or merely charged very high premiums will in many cases lead to the same result (since many people cannot afford high premiums) – an uninsured, high-risk population.

For some, or perhaps most, genetic diseases, genetics and medicine will have developed cures or at least remedial or prophylactic measures, thus shrinking the group of uninsurable individuals. Some of these therapies will probably be expensive, however, at least to start with. Insurance to cover the cost of such therapies will therefore be too expensive for a large part of the population, or else insurance companies will include clauses in their contracts to exclude cover for these diseases. This will leave people not uninsured, but underinsured, and more specifically uninsured against the disease for which they primarily need cover.[6] Even the most optimistic scenario concerning the development of genetics will probably not completely avoid the problem of an uninsured high-risk population, given absence of regulation.

This need not be a great problem, if private insurance is not vital to people's welfare (e.g. their access to health care, or their ability to guarantee that their children are provided for in case of death). If the dismantling of the social insurance systems keeps going, however, private insurance may become vital to people's welfare. This, we have claimed, is what is in fact happening (see chapter 4, section 4.4). One way to avoid the problem of an uninsured high-risk population that lacks access to vital goods, then, is to regulate insurance companies' access to genetic information, so that it cannot be used to identify the high-risk population. Total regulation may therefore appear to be a swift solution to this problem. As always, however, things are more complicated than that.

7.2.2   *Negative consequences of total regulation: adverse selection*

The problem of adverse selection is one of those most discussed with regard to the question of the access of insurance companies to genetic information. It is often considered to be the strongest argument in favour of insurance companies' right to genetic information, and thereby against total regulation (Sandberg, 1995, p. 1555). The problem is caused by the fact that the insurance seeker can use information to which the insurance company does not have access (asymmetric information, chapter 3, section 3.3.1) to buy an insurance policy on terms the insurance company would not have accepted if it too had had access to the information.[7] Genetic information that reveals a risk of disease or premature death is an example of such information. The problem of adverse selection then only arises from asymmetric information and so can only be used as an argument against total, and not partial, regulation (since partial regulation demands disclosure of genetic information possessed by the insurance applicant upon request).

---

[6] This is already a serious problem in the United States, where private and job-based health insurance often includes exclusionary clauses for serious long-term diseases. See e.g. Kass, 1997, pp. 308 f.; and Beauchamp and Childress, 2001, pp. 240 f.

[7] The international praxis is that insurance companies have a legal right to all information that is relevant in assessing the risk of an insurance policy (see ch. 3, section 3.1, and Chadwick and Ngwena, 1995, p. 120).

The severity of the problem of adverse selection depends on several crucial factors, of which the following are the most important: (i) the extent to which persons at high risk of genetic disease will use their knowledge of this to purchase insurance policies with high benefits without revealing the risk (that is, the extent to which the phenomenon of adverse selection is a real phenomenon);[8] (ii) the size of the detectable genetic risk, which depends on how many diseases can be predicted with genetic testing, how common these are and how much treatment and compensation for them cost (see chapter 2); (iii) the extent to which higher premiums for other insurance customers will make them take their business elsewhere or refrain altogether from insurance, which in turn depends on several, to some degree correlated, variables, such as the size of the rise in premium (which depends on the factors already mentioned), access to lower-cost premiums (which depends on the presence or absence of monopolies and cartels, among other things) and to what extent there is public insurance; and (iv) the form of insurance. The size of the compensation provided by a health insurance policy is in part determined by the cost of treatment, which depends on established medical practice (even if different treatments with different costs may exist). The size of the compensation provided is less limited by such external factors in the case of insurance for premature death. When it comes to such insurance the chances of using information to buy insurance with very high benefits are therefore greater and adverse selection a graver potential problem.

There are forces at work that give us good reason to believe that adverse selection may become a serious problem in the long run. As the analysis in chapter 5 demonstrated, the problem of adverse selection can, by a dynamic process, step by step, become so severe as to threaten the supply of personal private insurance altogether in countries where total regulation is implemented. One reaction might be, why should this be a concern? 'Let them scorch under the regulation fire.' One could regard other values, such as privacy, as being too important to justify caving in to the business interest of insurance companies.

Unfortunately there are more interests at stake than just the profit of a few insurance companies. Insurance companies contribute to the economy of a society, and hence indirectly to its welfare. Moreover, and

---

[8] If we allow generalisation from diseases other than genetic ones, there seems to be some evidence indicating that HIV has led to adverse selection (Chadwick and Ngwena, 1995, p. 119). However, research on females tested positive for BRCA1 shows very weak support for a correlation between positive tests and the number of life insurance policies (Smith et al., 1999). Nevertheless, there are known cases of persons testing positively for Huntington's disease who have applied for life insurance with very high benefits, and this may be taken as proof enough (Geller et al., 1996, p. 82).

more importantly, insurance is a good that is in demand, and all those demanding it will lack a matching supply if insurance companies are put out of business. This may not be a serious problem if the demand is a demand for a luxury good that one can well do without. The problem here is that this process may be combined with a dismantling of the social insurance system, leaving the same people uninsured as in the scenario without regulation. The regulation will then give rise to the same problem that it was intended to solve. We are faced with an emerging dilemma.

The dilemma is that whether insurance companies are permitted or prohibited the use of genetic information, the result may be an uninsured high-risk population – a 'genetic proletariat' (Billings *et al.*, 1992). In the case of being permitted to do so, this is because insurance companies will have an opportunity to differentiate premiums to the detriment of genetically high-risk persons. In the case of prohibition, it is because insurance companies are unable to differentiate premiums, which can make life and health insurance bad business. This dilemma has been called 'the Genetic Catch-22' and has been concisely summed up in these words: 'If insurers act, or are forced to act, generously by not using genetic testing, then they produce disastrous consequences; if they act selfishly and exclude clients on the basis of testing, then again, they produce disastrous consequences' (Hedgecoe, 1996, pp. 76 f.).

One way out of this dilemma is to implement partial regulation, that is, to allow insurance companies to ask for the results of previous tests, but not to demand new ones. This would limit the uninsured population to those who have already taken genetic tests that show a heightened risk of disease (excluding the possibility of preventive measures that will reduce the risk enough to make the price sufficiently low). In order to avoid this fate, individuals need only to refrain from taking such tests. Partial regulation, moreover, would prevent adverse selection, since it would make it illegal for the insurance seeker to withhold relevant genetic information if the insurance company asks for it (failure to disclose such information would make the contract invalid and leave the insurance company without any obligation to pay compensation). This would counteract the problem of asymmetric information, which is necessary for adverse selection.

7.2.3   Negative consequences of partial regulation: deterrence

Partial regulation, unfortunately, will probably have adverse consequences in terms of welfare, namely for those who have good reason to take a genetic test but have not yet done so. There may be several reasons for an individual to take an interest in information about his genetic constitution. One obvious reason is related to the individual's health. If he knows that he is at a higher risk of developing diabetes or high cholesterol because of his genetic constitution, this may influence him to change his lifestyle so as to avoid health problems. Another example is preventive measures to avoid some forms of genetically caused cancer (see chapter 2, section 2.2). Some of the individuals concerned may be able to reduce their risk enough by these measures to make them insurable. However, a further condition for making them insurable again is that the costs of treatment and income compensation are low enough. Since many genetic diseases are both severe and long-term, this condition will not be met in many cases.

Yet another reason for obtaining genetic information is in order to be able to plan one's life and one's reproductive decisions in the face of knowledge about genetic susceptibility to disease. These reasons for genetic testing hold whether or not there are preventive measures that can be taken against the disease.

However, some people may prefer to remain in ignorance concerning their genetic constitution, even if such knowledge is of vital importance to their health and life, rather than take the risk of being denied insurance (or being forced to pay premiums they cannot afford) if the test reveals a risk of disease. This deterrence to testing is of course a negative consequence for those individuals who would benefit from genetic testing in terms of welfare and/or autonomy.

How widespread is the problem of deterrence? This, obviously, is an empirical matter. No systematic scientific investigations have been made. However, some anecdotal evidence for the occurrence of the phenomenon does seem to be forthcoming. A reasonable conjecture is that the severity of the deterrence problem is dependent on the extent and generosity of the social insurance system. The more generous the public social system is, the less people will have to rely on private insurance to guard against misfortunes. In such a society, private personal insurance will be an expendable form of luxury commodity, with limited impact on general welfare. But where social insurance systems are not so generous (as in the United States and increasingly also in Europe), and where access to private insurance is a necessary means of access to other vital goods, such as health care, the reluctance to gather genetic information that can leave one uninsured is probably greater. In other words, the more important private insurance is to the individual's welfare, the greater the problem of deterrence will be, and the former factor is heavily dependent upon the presence of social insurance systems.[9]

---

[9] Not even generous social insurance systems, such as the Swedish, seem to avoid the deterrence problem altogether, however. So the problem is not to be underestimated. Genetic

To avoid the problem of deterrence, then, two different institutional arrangements are possible: to implement (or resurrect or sustain) generous social insurance systems or to implement total regulation, that is, ban access to genetic information altogether. The first option runs counter to what seems to be the trend in developed countries around the north Atlantic (chapter 4). This will lead to increasing problems for the second solution: the more people depend upon private insurance, the more acute the problem of adverse selection will be if total regulation is applied. Nevertheless, a combination of dismantling collective social insurance systems and bringing in stern regulation is the policy many of these countries have chosen. We have seen the problems this may lead to in terms of welfare.

The compromise chosen by, for example, Sweden may appear to solve both the problem of adverse selection and deterrence. As mentioned above (chapter 3, section 3.2.3), you are free to keep genetic information to yourself as long as insurance cover remains under a pre-specified amount and insurance companies are never allowed to demand new tests. The problem is that this creates another dilemma. The higher the pre-specified amount is set, the less the problem of deterrence, but the greater the problem of adverse selection. The lower the pre-specified amount is set, the less the problem of adverse selection, but the greater the problem of deterrence. Moreover, if the pre-specified amount is not high enough, the compensation may not be sufficient to cover the costs of health care and the loss of income for the sick person. All this, again, assumes the ongoing dismantling of collective insurance.

7.2.4   Consequentialism: summary

To summarise this section, there are reasons to believe that all types of regulation will lead to severe adverse consequences in terms of welfare. The form of regulation that seems to avoid the problem of an uninsured high-risk population more than any alternative form is partial regulation (which both avoids adverse selection and allows non-tested high-risk persons to buy insurance at a normal premium). However, partial regulation may be a deterrence to genetic testing, which can be a great loss.

---

counsellors have claimed that genetic testing has been aborted on several occasions because of fears concerning lack of private personal insurance (personal information from Christian Munthe, who is currently conducting an investigation on the subject in Swedish cancer clinics). In the United States there is even stronger evidence that the fear of a lack of insurance protection makes people reluctant to undergo genetic testing, which supports the line of argument above ('Bush Administration Backs Genetic Discrimination Ban', Memorandum from US administration, 13 February 2002, displayed on the Internet).

Moreover, it can still result in a group of persons who are unable to insure themselves. A social security system that is generous enough to make access to private insurance superfluous to basic welfare needs will, however, lessen these negative consequences of partial regulation.

7.3   Autonomy

7.3.1   Introduction

'People have a right to decide whether they want to be informed about their genetic constitution or not. This right is based on the principle of autonomy' (Sandberg, 1995, p. 1555). The statement represents a recurring opinion: considerations of autonomy provide a strong argument for the right to remain in ignorance of one's genetic constitution (Husted, 1997, pp. 63 f.; Takala, 2000, p. 79), and this provides a case against insurance companies making genetic testing a condition for insurance. In other words, autonomy at least speaks against absence of regulation (even if it may be consistent with only partial regulation).

The right to remain ignorant regarding one's genetic constitution seems to imply that insurance companies should not be allowed to demand new genetic tests as a condition for insurance, since genetic testing would reveal the individual's genetic constitution to him. Even if insurance companies were to refrain from disclosing the information to the applicant, the result would be indirectly revealed by the size of the insurance premium (or the denial of insurance altogether). The crucial question here is whether the right to autonomy justifies the right to remain in ignorance and whether this right is strong enough to override insurance companies' interest in genetic information. We will address this question later on (section 7.3.3).

Autonomy is, like justice (section 7.5.1), a concept that is positively value-laden and has a debatable meaning.[10] The etymology of the word, however, reveals that it has something to do with self-determination. We will use a minimalistic definition of autonomy (or self-determination) as a point of departure: to be autonomous is (at least) to decide what you want and to do what you decide (Tännsjö, 1998, p. 97).[11] In terms of

---

[10] See Dworkin, 1988, for a discussion of different theories of autonomy.

[11] This concept of autonomy can be interpreted as being incompatible with an orthodox Kantian concept, since Kant was of the opinion that empirical desires could never be the basis of autonomous decisions. The 'want' in the definition here presented should, however, be understood in a looser sense that is open to additional conditions (for instance, the Kantian condition that the choice is made out of respect for the law of practical reason).

this definition, various conflicting ideals of autonomy can be formulated that incorporate different opinions about the deontic status of autonomy (e.g. whether it is a restriction on what others may do to you, a value to be promoted or a duty to fulfil), and different views on how 'basic' it is (whether it is the goal of all action, an intrinsic value of some sort – a positive value to promote or a negative value to respect – or an instrumental value), why it is a value, and so on.

The concept of autonomy is intimately linked to the concept of freedom or liberty. Autonomy and liberty are often defended as prime values for human beings (Tännsjö, 1998, pp. 96 ff.). Defenders of autonomy often claim that self-determination is of supreme value to the individual, even if other people know better than the individual himself what would be best for him. The individual should have the liberty to make important decisions for himself, without being manipulated or interfered with.

In order to be autonomous an individual thus has to be able to make decisions and to act according to them.[12] To be able to make decisions he has to be able to evaluate different possible courses of action in terms of probable outcomes and the value of these outcomes in the light of his beliefs and desires. This requires the capability to imagine non-present possibilities, and to do so in a consistent fashion. Hence, it is necessary to have a certain amount of consciousness and reason to be able to act autonomously. Also, internal contradictions,[13] obsessions and confusion can make the individual unable to do so. One can also formulate ideals of autonomy that demand more of wishes and beliefs than consistency (see section 7.3.3). One can argue that the better informed the individual is, the more capable he is of making decisions in line with his own basic wishes, since he is more likely to succeed in realising his wishes if the beliefs he acts from are well-founded. This makes autonomy a matter of degree: generally, the more information relevant to a decision one has when making it, the more autonomous it is. From this point of view it seems difficult to defend a *general* right to ignorance.

To be able to act on one's decisions it is necessary not to be prevented by others from doing so. Sometimes support from others may be necessary in order to carry out the decisions one has made. Different ideals of

---

[12] To these two conditions a condition of authenticity can be added: that in order for the action to be autonomous, the wishes according to which the relevant decision is made should be formed independently by the agent himself. We will ignore this complication in the following discussion and simply assume that various such demands can be added to the ideals discussed, according to the reader's own approved view of autonomy.

[13] Two beliefs are contradictory if it is impossible for both of them (or the logical consequences of both) to be true, and two wishes if it is impossible to realise one of them given that the other has been realised, and vice versa.

autonomy demand different degrees of support from others (see section 7.3.3).[14]

Various mutually inconsistent ideals of autonomy can thus be formulated. In some such ideals, emphasis is put on the right of the individual not to be prevented by others from making decisions and acting on them, at least as long as the individual is not harming anyone else. According to this view autonomy can be defended on the grounds of the beneficial consequences of a generally respected right of this kind (Mill, 1859; Tännsjö, 1999). Others have claimed that it is bad in itself that the decisions of others are not respected (Glover, 1977, p. 84 f.) or that being autonomous is of value in itself (Kant, 1785; Nozick, 1974, p. 44 f.). Kant was even of the opinion that we have a duty to be autonomous: we should rule ourselves as far as possible, since the ability to do so is what separates us from the rest of nature and renders us our dignity.[15]

Because of the various possible ideals of autonomy, there is no easy way of establishing what rights can be defended with reference to autonomy. Autonomy has been referred to in order to defend both the right to know and the right not to know about one's genetic constitution,[16] as well as the duty to know about it, at least sometimes (which, of course, is incompatible with a right not to know).[17] It would demand at least a whole separate book to try to work out the implications of all these different ideals for insurance companies' rights to genetic information. Instead, we will focus upon two important ideals of autonomy that seem to lurk in the background of many arguments in this particular context, to see

[14] The difference between, on the one hand, not being prevented from performing an action one has decided on, and, on the other hand, being given a real opportunity to realise an alternative one considers desirable (with the help of others if needed), is sometimes described as a difference between two concepts of liberty: the negative and the positive (Berlin, 1958). Whether the difference is described as a difference in concept or ideal is a terminological matter that we will not go into further.

[15] See Kant, 1785. His concept or ideal of autonomy is different from most others, since he equates autonomy with acting in a manner free of any influences other than practical reason or the Categorical Imperative. To act autonomously is then the same thing as acting out of duty or in a morally praiseworthy manner. Most modern ideals of autonomy do not hold that an autonomous life also has to be a morally praiseworthy one.

[16] The Danish philosopher Husted, who has used autonomy to defend a right not to know, writes: 'Taking the decision of whether to know or not to know out of the person's hand is a case of doing the wrong thing, being a clear case of usurpation of decision making . . . The fact that the person receives new and relevant information does not in itself justify a claim of enhancement of autonomy' (Husted, 1997, p. 63).

[17] The American philosopher Rhodes, who has defended the view that there can be a duty to know about one's genetic constitution with reference to Kant's ideal of autonomy, writes: 'If autonomy justifies my right to knowledge, it cannot also justify my refusing to be informed . . . As sovereign over myself I am obligated to make thoughtful and informed decisions without being swayed by irrational emotions, including my fear of knowing significant genetic facts about myself' (Rhodes, 1998, p. 18).

whether they support the alleged conclusion that autonomy speaks in favour of partial regulation (at least).

7.3.2   Mill's ideal of autonomy

John Stuart Mill's famous ideal is that the autonomy of the individual should be respected, that is, he should not be prevented from acting according to his decisions and deciding according to his own wishes, at least as long as the actions do not harm anyone else (Mill, [1859] 1974, p. 68). For our autonomy to be violated according to this ideal, someone has thus actively to prevent us from making the decisions we want or from acting as we have decided. Would a demand from insurance companies for genetic testing constitute such a violation?

The following example suggests that it would not. Jack makes an unforced decision to take out life insurance. This insurance is sold in a market in which every personal insurance company demands genetic testing from the applicant, as part of the insurance contract. Jack, however, does not want to know about his genetic constitution. There is Huntington's disease in the family, and he knows that if he were to learn that he was a carrier of that hereditary disease, he would not be able to complete the great novel he is writing (one of his most important projects), due to the emotional paralysis that this knowledge would bring on him. Does this mean that the insurance companies are violating Jack's autonomy in a Millian sense?

The line of argument that suggests that this is not the case goes something like this. The right to have your decisions respected does not imply a right to get all you want on your own terms. The important point, according to this ideal of autonomy, is that you decide for yourself *given* the options you have. In the above situation, Jack can independently decide *either* to take out a life insurance policy *or* to remain in ignorance of his genetic constitution. Granted, he cannot decide to satisfy both these wishes. That, however, does not imply that the insurance companies are violating his autonomy, as understood by this ideal. Jack's autonomy is violated no more than Jill's would be if she were prevented from getting all the fishing tackle she wants, having already spent her money on rare Beatles records that she also wants. Considering market prices, Jill cannot get all she wants, yet this does not mean that the salesmen of the city have violated her autonomy.

In an analogy with Jill's case, Jack's autonomy is also not violated because of the obstacles he is subject to. Buying insurance is an economic transaction, where the buyer chooses to accept or reject the terms of the seller (Borna and Avila, 1999, p. 357). As long as these choices are respected, there is no violation of autonomy, according to Mill. It would be strange to claim that insurance companies actively prevent Jack from deciding what he wants and doing what he decides to do, simply by setting terms that Jack does not accept. Even if Jack then chooses not to acquire something he would have acquired if the terms had been more beneficial (that is, if insurance companies did not demand genetic testing), we cannot say that insurance companies thereby actively harm Jack (which could have been an argument for regulating insurance companies' terms, according to Mill). Accordingly, Mill's famous ideal of autonomy cannot be used as an argument in favour of even partial regulation.

7.3.3   Autonomy as self-realisation

Mill's ideal of autonomy is not so much a question of degree.[18] Our autonomy is violated when someone actively prevents us from putting our own decisions into effect, even though no harm to others would result from our doing so. If we are not so prevented, our autonomy is respected. The purpose of this ideal is to stake out the limits of a private sphere, within which no one may interfere and which ideally gives us the opportunity to realise our plans.

However, this may seem insufficient. Most people are interested in real, and not just formal, opportunities to realise (from their point of view) important plans and wishes. For this to be possible some may need more than non-interference: they may need active help from someone else. If autonomy is of value, it may therefore seem that people in such situations have at least a prima facie claim on others to receive such help (if they so wish). While this fuller ideal of autonomy can come in many variations (depending on the status and weight assigned to the value of autonomy), the basic idea is easy enough to state: to the extent that the individual is leading his life according to his basic ideals and plans (or projects or goals), he is autonomous. In other words: to be autonomous is to live life according to one's own standards. Therefore, we all have a reason not just to refrain from the 'active' infringement of other people's autonomy, but to actively *promote* their autonomy as well, that is, to take active measures to ensure that people have real opportunities to live their lives according to their own standards (at least as long as living such a life does not prevent anyone else from doing the same). This is therefore called the ideal of self-realisation.[19] This ideal of course says something

---

[18] Other interpretations of Mill are of course possible.

[19] This term may be used to designate several different ideas, which are not to be confused with the present one. The present idea is not that we should realise inborn talents and

more than that a person's decisions should be respected (at least if they really match that person's wants and their realisation does not actively harm anyone else) – it says that it is of value to be autonomous and that this value can be promoted by people other than the individual himself (only the individual himself can ultimately decide to live autonomously, but others can help him to make this a real possibility). This idea of autonomy is often discussed by medical ethicists (Glover, 1984, p. 160; Harris, 1998, p. 148; Munthe, 1999, p. 198) and has also been referred to as the one providing justification for genetic testing (Munthe, 1999, p. 84).

The ideal of self-realisation takes autonomy to be a question of degree to a greater extent than does Mill's ideal. We can be more or less autonomous depending on our competence to make our own decisions and our ability to implement them. Genetic information can enhance our capacity to lead more autonomous lives and, according to this ideal, then, this constitutes a reason for providing such testing. The following example can serve as an illustration. Peter suspects that he has the genetic damage causing Huntington's disease, since his father has recently died as a result of it (which gives him a 50 per cent risk of being a carrier of the gene). Peter is also facing an important career choice, and his life expectancy is crucial for what he will think he should choose. Until now, his mind was set on a lengthy education, which would enable him to make a good living later on in life. But now he is seriously considering staying at his present job (which he likes) and instead spending more time on his hobby. A genetic test can obviously help Peter to make a well-founded decision on the basis of his own wishes in this case.

However, it is more reasonable to claim that a demand from insurance companies that applicants take genetic tests is detrimental to autonomy interpreted as an ideal of self-realisation rather than as interpreted according to Mill's ideal. Let us turn once more to Jack to show this. Although it is still reasonable to claim that insurance companies do not force Jack to take a genetic test by demanding this as a term of contract, this demand nevertheless limits Jack's opportunities to realise his important plans. The severity of the limitation depends on Jack's plans and the circumstances under which Jack makes his choice. If the circumstances are such that there is an asymmetry of power to Jack's disadvantage, the severity increases. This is true if he needs the insurance more than the insurance company needs him as a customer (his bargaining position is

possibilities, which is considered valuable whether the individual in fact values such a realisation and makes it a project or not. This last ideal is sometimes called perfectionism (Tännsjö, 1998, p. 87), and is usually ascribed to Marx and Aristotle.

then worse than if the reverse were true). This is more likely to be the case if there are very meagre collective social insurance systems. Let us picture a society where Jack's children are dependent on life insurance to be able to continue their education in the event of his premature death. If one of his most important plans – other than to finish the great novel – is to provide for his children, then given such circumstances, his chances of living autonomously are severely limited by the insurance companies' demands. If private life insurance on the other hand is an expendable commodity whose purpose would be to make the children rich in the case of his premature death, then the severity of the limitation lessens.

What is valid for Jack is also valid on a general level: the extent to which insurance companies' demands for genetic testing limit people's autonomy depends on people's values and plans and the circumstances under which they choose. To what extent are the demands of insurance companies incompatible with the plans of people in general? To be able to answer this, we must be familiar with society's basic social institutions, the values and projects that are most important and widespread among the population (which requires intimate knowledge about the culture), and so on. If it is shown that the demands of insurance companies to use genetic information really limit the individual's opportunities for self-realisation, does this mean that the companies should be forbidden to demand such information? The answer depends on the kind of value we ascribe to autonomy as self-realisation: the greater its value, the more reason we have to restrict demands from insurance companies (or anyone else) that will impede the realisation of this value.

How great is the value of living your life according to your own basic values and wishes, then? We think that no one would say that this is of no value whatsoever, but different ethical theories will provide different answers as to how great this value is and why. Consequentialism, as defined here, gives self-realisation an instrumental value. The value of self-realisation depends on the contribution that self-realisation makes to welfare. According to the hedonistic version of consequentialism, the value of self-realisation partly depends on how much people would suffer from the prospect of not being able to live according to their own values and plans. In our society, this suffering is probably worse than in societies with fewer or other expectations of life. To cut a long story short, a consequentialist must know about all manner of things in order to determine the value of self-realisation.

Other theories assign intrinsic value to autonomy in this sense. Modern liberals[20] especially seem inclined to do so. If self-realisation is of intrinsic

---

[20] Like Rawls and Nozick. See ch. 7, sections 7.2 and 7.5.3.2.

value, it must be of equal value to all individuals (what grounds could there be to claim that my self-realisation is of greater value than yours or vice versa?). Hence, we should all have equal opportunity to realise our projects and live according to our values (this is, obviously, along the lines of Rawls's reasoning in *A Theory of Justice*, 1972). The right of insurance companies to use genetic information should then be restricted to the extent that it limits possibilities of self-realisation, especially for those whose possibilities are already limited due to their genetic constitution. Unlike Mill's ideal of autonomy, this ideal will naturally raise questions of justice, since it makes it a duty to contribute to other people's self-realisation. Typical questions of justice then arise: who should contribute, how much, and to whom?

7.3.4   Autonomy: summary

Different ideals of autonomy support different conclusions concerning the regulation of insurance companies' access to and use of genetic information. Mill's ideal of autonomy cannot be used to defend any kind of regulation.[21] Autonomy interpreted as an ideal of self-realisation seems more promising as a basis for a defence of regulation. To use this ideal to support such a conclusion, we need to know a great deal; we need to know about societal circumstances, people's plans and values, what kind of value autonomy is and how great its value. What kind of regulation it supports is therefore uncertain. The ideal speaks in favour of partial regulation to the extent that the right to demand genetic testing undermines the individual's opportunities to realise important plans and values. The argument could be used in favour of total regulation, for instance, if the problem of deterrence becomes so severe that people's opportunities to live the lives they choose are limited as a result (they may need genetic information about themselves to be able to live such lives). We must once again stress the significance of societal circumstances in addressing this issue. If society is so arranged that people do not need private insurance in order to gain access to important goods that are vital to opportunities in society (such as health care, education, etc.), then people will be able to realise important plans regardless of regulations affecting private insurance. Autonomy interpreted as an ideal of self-realisation can also be used as an argument for the supply of presymptomatic and predictive genetic testing, besides the arguments that refer to the existing and potential medical benefits of genetics.

---

[21] This does not imply that it supports absence of regulation. The correct conclusion is that it does not directly support any kind of regulation, nothing more.

7.4   Privacy

7.4.1   Introduction

The term privacy refers to a protected zone around the individual – a private sphere where the individual is especially entitled to non-interference from others as well as to control over what is happening. This sphere can be broad and general or just concern certain aspects of the individual (for instance the physical body), certain information or some kinds of decisions. The defence for such a private sphere has a long tradition in the legislation of Western civilisation (McGleenan, 1997, pp. 43 f.). For instance, it is common to refer to privacy when claiming the right to control information about oneself (e.g. information about one's sexual orientation or genetic constitution), to avoid interference with respect to certain decisions (e.g. about abortion), to avoid supervision (e.g. in public places), or not to answer certain questions (e.g. from one's employer about political opinions, recreational activities or reproductive plans).

Privacy is not equivalent to autonomy; the right sometimes to be 'left alone' does not in itself mean self-determination. But the right to privacy can be justified with reference to autonomy: to be able to practise self-determination it can be necessary to be left alone. Mill's ideal of autonomy can be seen as an attempt to defend privacy with reference to the value of autonomy (which in turn can be defended with reference to welfare, according to Mill): to be autonomous in any interesting sense we must demarcate a sphere where others in general, and society in particular, must not interfere.

The question in this context is whether genetic information should belong to such a protected sphere. Is there such a thing as *genetic* privacy? Is there anything special about an individual's genetic information that makes it especially worthy of protection?

First, let us add a few further points about privacy. How well protected should a piece of information be in order to be counted as part of a person's privacy? When is your privacy protected? Privacy as commonly understood seems to require a great deal of protection. Accepting this received opinion, we will say that genetic privacy is protected when the individual himself has full control over his genetic information, without running the risk of adverse consequences, whatever he chooses to do with it (at least as long as he does not use it to harm others). If he can be excluded from insurance because of reluctance to disclose genetic information to insurance companies, his genetic privacy is not being fully respected, according to this definition of privacy. A successful argument in favour of this strong form of privacy thus speaks in favour of total regulation as well.

7.4.2   Is there anything special about genetic information?

The question in this context is, then, the following: is there something special about genetic information that makes it an object for special concern in legislation and regulation? This is in effect – given the assumption made about there being ethical reasons for laws and other formal societal rules – to ask for the ethical significance of genetic information. Four main characteristics have been used to argue that genetic information is different from other (medical) information in morally relevant ways: genetic information is (i) predictive about disease before onset; (ii) transmittable to offspring; (iii) revealing about persons other than the one tested (namely, the person's relatives); and (iv) especially personal and intimate.

The received wisdom in today's discussion is that none of these characteristics single out genetic information as deserving special treatment compared with other medical information, not even when taken together (Holm, 1999; Launis, 2000; Sandberg, 1995, pp. 1550 ff.). This is because other non-genetic information is claimed to be relevantly similar. This does not show that genetic information should not be protected in the name of privacy, but that other information that is relevantly similar should be treated in the same way (this is the motivation in Norwegian legislation for prohibiting insurance companies from using any kind of medical information; see chapter 3, section 3.2.3). The point that other information is relevantly similar to genetic information is easily made as regards characteristics (i) to (iii). A great deal of non-genetic (medical) information is predictive about disease before onset, for example information about HIV carrier status, smoking and cholesterol. Many risk factors besides genes are transmitted to offspring, for example the HIV virus, the environment in the womb and social position.[22] Some non-genetic diseases reveal information about persons other than the one tested, for example sexually transmittable diseases. Information about HIV carrier status, for instance, thus shares all these characteristics with genetic information.

The most debated characteristic is the personal and intimate nature of genetic information. The argument should not rely on the highly

---

[22] Evidently, not all people have the same social position as their parents, but people have a higher probability of occupying the same social position (the social heritage). This also applies to genetic heritage, however.

controversial idea that there is something very personal about genetic information as such, since this claim would draw on a form of genetic essentialism that has already been refuted (chapter 2). A person neither is his genes nor is he determined solely by them. However, no one should deny that genetic information is considered to be very personal and private in our culture, as is information about sexual preference, private relations and so on.[23]

The fact that genetic information is considered personal and private can be used to argue that it should be protected. Laws of privacy are often justified with reference to the importance of respecting the feeling that this information is nobody else's business (chapter 3, section 3.4.2). These laws are then based on a broader utilitarian foundation. People feel distressed and worried about the fact that others may gain access to information they think of as very personal and private. This is one explanation of the fact that many are reluctant to share genetic information with third parties (Borna and Avila, 1999; Mayer et al., 1999). According to this line of reasoning, regulation of access to genetic information is justified because it helps people to protect the genetic information they would be distressed by if it were known to others. To put it more simply: why genetic privacy? To avoid distress and worry.

If there is nothing inherent in genetic information that makes it especially worthy of protection, and the reasons for protecting genetic privacy are general utilitarian ones, then the question arises as to how efficient the regulation of insurance companies' access to genetic information is as a means to utilitarian ends. Is regulation for the purpose of protecting genetic privacy an efficient means of handling people's distress? Some have claimed that such legislation can be counterproductive (McGleenan, 1997; Wolf, 1995). Regulation can contribute to the opinion that genetic information is a strange and potentially dangerous matter that we had better keep secret, and thus reinforce the ideology of genetic essentialism. Furthermore, if genetic conditions receive special regulatory treatment, we risk stigmatising further those affected by them. There is an analogy to a restrictive policy on immigration. Such a policy can be motivated by concern about the distress caused by encountering foreign cultures. The result is fewer encounters with foreign cultures, which will reinforce cultural prejudices, which in turn will increase the distress caused by encountering foreign cultures.

There are other measures that can be taken to prevent the distress caused by third party access to genetic information. One way is to offer

---

[23] However, what people consider to be very personal and private – what they feel is nobody else's business, so to speak – changes over time (ch. 3, section 3.4.2).

greater choice whether or not to reveal such information to third parties. In the case of insurance companies, this can be accomplished through public social security systems with a widened scope. Such a system allows the individual to choose not to disclose the information, without the risk of losing access to important basic goods, such as health care.

One important explanation for the great reluctance in the United States to accept insurance companies' access to genetic information is probably the fear of being left without insurance that is vital for health care and other important goods. Regulation may not be an efficient means of solving this problem. First, there is the problem of defining genetic information and genetic testing in such a way that regulation prevents their use. Even if we focus on monogenetic diseases, which are genetic in a straightforward way, these may be tested for by means other than genetic testing. Cystic fibrosis, for example, is tested for by using a chloride test on perspiration. Is this then genetic testing?

Second, there are properties other than genetic ones that insurance companies can and do use to demarcate genetically high-risk populations.[24] An illuminating analogy is the problem in the United States of using legislation to prevent discrimination by insurance companies against those who are HIV-positive. When the use of HIV tests was prevented, other medical tests (of T-cells) were used instead. When this was prohibited, insurance companies used sexual orientation to identify the relevant high-risk population. When this was regulated against, insurance companies began to differentiate against occupations where homosexuals were disproportionately represented, and so on (Rothstein, 1997, p. 471). Insurance companies are not interested in causal relations but in statistical correlations, and some features have to be singled out if private insurance is to be economically sustainable. The genetic case, of course, is even more problematic to regulate, because of the numerous ways in which such regulation can be sidestepped due to the range of diseases that are genetic.

7.4.3   Privacy: summary

Genetic privacy can be protected by total regulation. The primary reason for protecting genetic information is to avoid the distress that would be felt if it were not protected, since genetic information is considered personal and private. There are, however, problems in using regulation as a means of protecting genetic information. First, regulation may reinforce the fear

---

[24] One way is to use ethnic groups, as in the much-debated example of sickle-cell anaemia among the US black population in the 1960s (ch. 3, section 3.4.3).

of genetic information and further stigmatise genetically caused illness. Second, regulation may be an inefficient means of eliminating distress caused by the fear of being left without insurance, since insurance companies can use other than genetic criteria to single out genetically high-risk populations. Privacy can, however, be protected to a certain extent by means other than regulation. There is the possibility of guaranteeing access to vital goods without access to private insurance, through a social insurance system, thus without revealing genetic information and providing protection of privacy. Such a system would make genetic information less dramatic and thus counteract the belief in genetic essentialism, which would be a gain.

7.5   Justice

7.5.1   Introduction

Justice is one of the basic concepts of ethics in general and of political philosophy in particular. Like autonomy, the concept of justice has a debatable meaning, but is always positively valued. That is to say, everyone agrees that justice is a good thing, but there is fierce disagreement about what is just. Justice is the most common consideration of a normative character brought to bear in the discussion on insurance companies' right to genetic information.

Sometimes it has been claimed that there are various ideals of justice, but one basic concept of justice on which the various ideals agree. This has been stated in numerous ways, with minor differences in substance.[25] It is, however, hard to find anything that is both unique and common to different ideas of justice. It has been claimed that all ideas of justice are ideas of equality (Dworkin, 1977, p. 179). This is true, at least on a very loose definition of equality, to the effect that *relevantly similar cases should be treated similarly* (this is known as the formal principle of justice). This means, for instance, that if some dividable good is to be distributed between two persons, and there is no difference between them of any relevance, from the point of view of justice they should each receive (or have) the same amount of the good.[26] However, this is unsatisfactory as

---

[25] See e.g. Hart, 1961, p. 156, who claims that justice has a core of meaning that is constant between different users; Rawls (1972, p. 5), who differentiates between a common *concept of justice* and different *conceptions of justice*; and Hare (1991, pp. 123 ff.), who differentiates between the formal principle of justice (relevantly similar cases should be treated similarly) and different substantial principles of justice.

[26] On this both Nozick and utilitarians can agree, since 'relevantly similar' in Nozick's terminology would mean 'equal entitlement' and if two people have entitlements to an

a unique characteristic of justice. First, it is close to empty, since one has not yet defined 'relevantly similar', and secondly, this may not differentiate principles of justice from other ethical principles (some would claim that this is nothing more than the principle of universalisability, which is common to all ethical judgements; see e.g. Hare, 1981).

Something more is thus required to demarcate questions of justice from other normative judgements. One such proposed characteristic is that questions of justice are questions of the distribution of benefits and burdens. There is no unanimity on this point,[27] but in this context it is a reasonable supposition. From the point of view of the insured, insurance (and genetic testing) can be considered as a benefit or a *good*, and premiums as a burden.[28] The situation is the reverse for insurance companies.[29] The question of justice, then, is how these goods and burdens should be distributed. The question in no way implies anything about there being a distributor (as regards private insurance, the market, not a sovereign state, takes care of distribution, according to the principles of supply and demand) or about the method of distribution. In some theories of justice, the method of distribution is relevant to the justice of the distribution (e.g. Nozick's theory), and these theories cannot be excluded without a hearing.

If we concentrate on goods (which is customary in discussions of justice), how are they to be distributed? The proposals as to what kinds of distribution are just are legion and (often) incompatible: distribution should be according to desert (Rachels, 1991), according to need (Miller, 1976), such that the situation of the worst off cannot be improved further (Rawls, 1972), such that welfare is maximised (total welfare: Hare, 1991; average welfare: Harsanyi, 1977),[30] the result of an unforced trade on a free market (Nozick, 1974), or the result of negotiation between the involved parties (Gauthier, 1986). To complicate matters further, propositions have been made that different principles should be applied to different goods (Walzer, 1983). Indeed, the nature of the goods to

equal amount of a dividable good, they should each receive the same amount. A similar reasoning is applicable to utilitarians, who would say that 'relevantly similar' amounts to something like 'has equal interest in' or 'maximises the happiness of the persons'.

[27] See Young, 1990.

[28] Insurance is often employer-based, especially health insurance in the United States (Beauchamp and Childress, 2001, p. 240). Here the employee does not pay premiums directly, but does so indirectly, since the insurance cover could otherwise have been given to the employee directly as salary.

[29] Strictly speaking, insurance does not have to be a burden to insurance companies (it is the commodity they are selling and want to sell, since this gives them their profit). But paying compensation to the insured is.

[30] These principles amount to consequentialism as defined here, and will not be discussed as separate theories of justice.

be distributed is a controversial question (one that we fortunately do not have to address in this context, since this is defined by the subject matter).

Considering this multitude of principles, can there be any hope of saying anything definite about what is just? In most cases it is difficult. In the case of personal insurance, however, a grouping of principles along two major lines is feasible, as disagreement in theory does not necessarily preclude agreement in practice. This we will try to demonstrate in the following. *On the one hand* we have the principle of desert and various principles in favour of far-reaching equality in the distribution of the resources of society – principles that are therefore termed principles of equality (of which we will discuss three: the difference principle, the priority principle and the principle of need). These principles are sometimes used to argue against the right of insurance companies to genetic information, and in favour of total regulation. *On the other hand* there are principles that defend the right to keep things acquired through transactions and negotiations. These will be called principles of voluntariness and are used to argue for the right of insurance companies to ask for and use genetic information.

We will also discuss a third group of theories of justice that are relevant to this issue – theories that claim different principles of justice to be applicable in different circumstances. We will examine the most elaborate version of such theories, namely Walzer's theory of complex equality. This theory can be described as an attempted compromise between principles of equality and principles of voluntariness.

Contrary to what has been suggested in the debate, the principle of desert and the principles of equality do not directly support total regulation. Rather, they support a more general conclusion that is noncommittal regarding more specific practical arrangements, namely, that no one should suffer an excessive burden because of his genetic constitution. Rather, genetic susceptibility to disease is a ground for compensation, according to these views. This conclusion is neutral as regards the method by which such compensation should be accomplished. Principles of voluntariness are either implausible (which is shown for instance by their application to this case) or else fail to support the libertarian conclusions they are claimed to uphold. The most reasonable application of Walzer's theory of justice will reach conclusions similar to the principles of equality, since private personal insurance is increasingly becoming a good that is necessary to security and welfare and such goods, the theory states, should be distributed according to need. Consequently, reasonable considerations of justice all agree on the claim that burdens due to one's genetic constitution are grounds for compensation.

Table 7.1. *The principles of justice discussed*

Principle of justice	Definition	What it supports
Principle of desert	Distribution according to desert (advantages according to beneficial consequences the person is responsible for, and burdens, e.g. punishment, according to adverse consequences the person is responsible for)	Total regulation
Difference principle	Distribution to the advantage of the worst off	Total regulation
Priority principle	Distribution to the advantage of the worse off	Total regulation
Principle of need	Distribution according to need	Total regulation
Actuarial fairness	Distribution (of premiums) according to risk	Absence of regulation
Libertarianism	Distribution according to voluntary exchange of justly acquired property	Absence of regulation
Complex equality	Distribution according to the social meaning of the good	Regulation, partial or total

The numerous principles of justice that will be discussed in the following may confuse a reader not familiar with these theories beforehand. We will therefore present table 7.1, listing the most important principles, along with short definitions and their views on regulation. As has already been mentioned, the views on regulation presented should not be taken as the views actually implied by the principles. Rather, they are the views that have been argued for with reference to these principles or the views that these principles seem to support prima facie. The first four principles in the table will be discussed in section 7.5.2, the two following in section 7.5.3 and the last in 7.5.4.

7.5.2   *Justice: desert and equality*

Is a practice that allows insurance companies the right to ask for genetic information just? An argument that seems to tell against this is that no one should have to suffer from misfortunes for which he himself cannot reasonably be held responsible (Dworkin, 1985, p. 207; Rawls, 1972, pp. 47 f.; Roemer, 1995, pp. 4 f.). On the basis of this *principle of desert* the following can be argued (Holtug, 1999, pp. 284 ff.). We can only be held responsible for that which we ourselves choose (or for the foreseeable consequences of such choices). No one chooses his or her own genetic constitution. It is therefore not just that someone who has suffered ill fortune in the natural lottery by inheriting an increased susceptibility to disease should on this account suffer from limited access to or denial of other goods, such as insurance. On the contrary, such a person should rather be compensated for those burdens that are due to his misfortune.[31] If insurance companies are allowed access to genetic information, they will exclude from insurance the people already burdened by undeserved bad luck, precisely because of their bad luck (i.e. their increased susceptibility to disease). Therefore the companies should not have access to this information. The prima facie impression, then, might be that the principle of desert speaks in favour of total regulation (Johnston, 1999, pp. 80, 83 f.).

The principle of desert is often linked to the ideal of equal opportunities. The reasoning behind this ideal goes something along the following lines. In modern societies of the Western type, there is competition for favoured positions – favoured in that they entail an advantageous allocation of basic goods, such as income and status (one of the bases for self-respect). In order for this competition to be just, we must all have equal opportunities to succeed in it; circumstances must not be to anyone's disadvantage. There are basically four different views on how circumstances can be seen as equalised in order to make opportunities equal: (i) the absence of legal barriers to favoured positions (e.g. no nobles; formal equal opportunities); (ii) the elimination of informal barriers based on gender, ethnicity, sexual orientation and so on; (iii) the elimination of all social circumstances that have consequences for competition but that are not the result of the competitors' own choices (i.e., elimination of the social lottery); and (iv) the elimination of all circumstances, natural and social, that have consequences for competition but are not the result of the competitors' own choices.[32]

It has been claimed that we have equal opportunities in a morally non-arbitrary way only when we have reached step (iv) in the equalising of opportunities (Rawls, 1972, p. 74; Roemer, 1995, pp. 2 f.). At that point people's positions are determined by their own choices, rather than circumstances they cannot do anything about. When we have eliminated the

---

[31] Holtug, 1999, however, argues that an extra premise (such as a principle of equality) is needed to reach the conclusion that undeserved burdens should be compensated (p. 287). He does not claim that the principle of desert implies that regulation should be implemented.

[32] The first three steps can be found in Buchanan et al., 2000, p. 65. Including the fourth step we have the view of equal opportunity that they call the 'brute luck' view.

effects of such natural and social circumstances, what we have left is the individual's own contribution. This is what the person is entitled to, is justified in claiming or deserves. Interpreted in this way, the principle of desert leads to far-reaching equality: no one should have to suffer severe detrimental consequences because of things he himself cannot do anything about. However, this leaves two questions open for interpretation, first, what should be counted as 'severe detrimental consequences' (who are to be compensated?), and, second, how this compensation should be accomplished in a society with scarce resources. Here, more substantial theories of equality come into play. In the following we will consider three main versions of such theories: the difference principle, the priority principle and the principle of need.

Rawls's difference principle is so widely discussed that a more detailed presentation than the following is unnecessary: 'social primary goods . . . are to be distributed equally unless an unequal distribution . . . is to the advantage of the least favoured' (1972, p. 303). We will not account for the argumentation that leads to this principle or explicate the principle further, since that is unnecessary for our purposes. Only the application of Rawls's conception or ideal of justice to the question of the right of insurance companies to genetic information is of primary interest here. This brings into focus the basic moral intuition that this ideal of justice expresses: the claim that we have special obligations towards those worst or worse off.

Rawls's theory of justice nevertheless has many inherent problems that should not be disregarded. One problem is the difficulty of identifying the worst-off group (is it made up of a small destitute minority or of everyone but the best off, or something in between?).[33] Besides that, the privileged position that Rawls gives this group has troubling consequences, in that the least improvement for the worst off always outweighs an improvement for the second worst-off group, no matter the size of the improvement for this group, the size of the groups and no matter even if the difference between the groups is very small to start with (Holtug, 1999, p. 288). These consequences are to some extent the result of Rawls's concentration on groups instead of individuals, but also of his stern deontological reluctance to balance the interest of the worst off against the interests of others.

The more general moral intuition reflected by Rawls's theory of justice, however, does not have to solve these kinds of technicalities. It is enough

---

[33] Rawls has some, though not very well elaborated, suggestions as to how this should be done (but not very much about why it should be done in the way in which he proposes), 1972, p. 98.

to claim that the worse off someone is, the stronger the obligation of others to help him. This general idea is summed up by the *priority principle*: 'Benefiting people matters more [morally] the worse off these people are' (Parfit, 1997, p. 213). This principle can be used to argue against insurance companies' right to genetic information, since this right would often be used to the disadvantage of the already badly off individual (Holtug, 1999, p. 290). People who already suffer from a natural disadvantage (the increased risk of developing disease) are further burdened by reduced opportunities to insure themselves against this, a fact that seems to be contrary to the priority principle.

Similar reasoning seems applicable to the *principle of need*: we should receive goods according to need. What need is, when someone is needy and what determines the extent of a need, is notoriously hard to define (Kymlicka, 1990, pp. 183 ff.). The spirit of the principle of need is, however, congenial to the priority principle; to be worse off is often to be needy in the sense in which this word is commonly used. Those in most need of insurance will be the people suffering the greatest difficulty in obtaining it. Any reasonable interpretation of the principle of need might therefore seem to favour the same conclusion as the priority principle: total regulation.

In spite of the apparent force of these lines of reasoning, however, the conclusion is premature. The principles of equality do indeed demand that those suffering from misfortunes, such as genetically caused disease, should be compensated as far as is possible. The more fortunate have an obligation to give up some of their goods to help those worse off, even if this causes a decrease in the net balance of goods. All this speaks in favour of a redistribution to the benefit of those unfortunate individuals. But it does not tell us that insurance companies form the party obliged to perform this redistribution. Rather, all of those who are better off should contribute.

Moreover, as we have seen, the effect of forcing insurance companies to provide for the genetically worse off by prohibiting insurance companies' use of genetic information may be the collapse of private personal insurance. The problem that regulation was intended to solve will then re-emerge, as a result of this very regulation. This consequence is also problematic to the principle of equality, since it would further burden an already burdened group.

There is a further problem in letting private insurance and regulation solve the problem of compensating the genetically worse off, namely, the problem of overcompensation. You might purchase a health insurance policy to guarantee access to proper care in case of disease or injury. You might also purchase it to save money or to acquire wealth. The worry of insurance companies is that persons allowed to withhold genetic risk will enter insurance contracts with very high benefits, not to guarantee a decent level of welfare, but to strike exceedingly rich. The same thing goes for premature death insurance, probably to an even greater extent.[34] The construction of such special opportunities seems difficult to defend with reference to considerations of justice. We may have an obligation to help people in need or to compensate for arbitrary inequalities, but we surely do not have any obligation to make persons with genetic disorders vastly richer than the average person. Any such policy might also undermine solidarity with this group.

All of these problems speak in favour of another solution to the problem of achieving justice (according to the principle of desert and the principles of equality) for the genetically high-risk group. The solution favoured should be familiar by now: a generous collective social insurance system that guarantees that no one stands helpless in case of disease.

7.5.3   Justice: voluntariness and rights

7.5.3.1 Actuarial fairness   Principles of justice have also been used as arguments for insurance companies' right to genetic information. The most frequent argument refers to the actuarial assessment of risk (Sandberg, 1995, p. 1554; Wortham, 1986, p. 361). The whole idea of private insurance is based on the assumption that people pay premiums in proportion to the risk of payment of insurance benefits taken by the company. With access to genetic information, insurance companies can take the higher risk posed by those with damaged genes into consideration, and differentiate premiums accordingly. The idea of actuarial fairness is, in line with the spirit of private insurance, that everyone should pay premiums according to his own risk, or to phrase it in negative terms, no one should have to pay a higher premium than is justified by the risk he actually represents. Justice according to actuarial fairness rests on 'the *moral* judgement that *fair underwriting* practices must reflect the division of people according to the *actuarially accurate* determination of their risks' (Daniels, 1990, p. 500, emphasis in original).

The concept of actuarial risk is problematic, however. As far as we know, no one has explicitly defended the view that the calculations of risk undertaken by insurance companies aim to reflect any kind of 'objective' risk or probability. Since it is highly debatable whether there is any such

---

[34] This is because the insurer and the insured have more freedom to set the terms of compensation when it comes to life insurance than in the case of health insurance. See chapter 2, section 2.3, and section 7.2.2 above. See also Chadwick and Ngwena, 1995, p. 123.

thing as objective probability (Resnik, 1997, p. 61), a defence of actuarial fairness would therefore benefit from avoiding relying on any such assumptions. A more promising interpretation of the concept of actuarial risk is to refer to the accurate calculation of risk, given the known factors relevant to the risk in question (Harper, 1993, p. 224).

However, insurance companies do not use all known factors relevant to the risk in question when they differentiate premiums. The calculation of risk and differentiation of premiums are based on a limited number of factors. To use all the known factors that are relevant for estimating the risk of disease and premature death would simply make the investigation of potential customers too expensive to bear its own costs. The customary procedure is, therefore, to use some factors traditionally seen as highly relevant, for which statistics are already available. Hence, all assessments of risk are more or less arbitrary in comparison with the actuarial ideal. The problem is not just that insurance companies defend a practice with reference to an ideal (actuarial fairness) that they do not attain. What is worse is that insurance companies do not even try to reach this ideal. They have other more important (economic) considerations that stand in the way. If the actuarial ideal can be so outweighed by these sorts of considerations from the point of view of the insurance companies, then it stands to reason that *all* claims based on actuarial fairness can be similarly outweighed. For example, they may be outweighed by economic factors affecting potential customers – such as the economic risk of undergoing or revealing the results of genetic testing.

All of this is, of course, compatible with the claim that actuarial fairness can in fact not be outweighed in this way, and that insurers should sacrifice the economic gains of applying cheap and simple methods of risk assessment for the sake of actuarial fairness. However, such a suggestion presupposes that the actuarial ideal expresses a fundamental tenet of justice, whereas in fact actuarial fairness, viewed as an independent principle of justice, has inherent problems. The ideal is based on a dubious moral principle: individuals should be able to gain from their natural advantages, even when others stand to lose because of this (we will later discuss libertarianism, which defends this position). This is contrary to the principles of equality previously discussed, according to which natural disadvantages are grounds for compensation rather than further burdens. If one finds such principles of justice reasonable, one cannot consistently embrace actuarial fairness.

However, against egalitarian theories of justice one can argue that it is reasonable that we at least sometimes should be allowed to gain benefits because of our natural advantages. This seems to be necessary in a market economy of the Western type. Theories of equality can, however, be compatible with this view. Even Rawls's outspoken egalitarianism agrees that people should be allowed to gain from natural advantages, but only in so far that this is to the benefit of the worst off. This may be the case if everybody in a society, including the worst off, stands to lose from blocking incentives to talent. In this particular case, however, the question is not whether or not we should forbid talented people to gain from their capacities. Instead, the question is whether those who suffer the bad luck of being genetically susceptible to disease should be further burdened by exclusion from other goods, such as health care. Since this may be a consequence of the principle of justice implied by actuarial fairness, most people will probably be reluctant to accept this as a reasonable principle.

A perhaps more convincing argument in favour of actuarial fairness instead refers to the fact that allowing people to withhold genetic information from insurance companies will force low-risk individuals to subsidise high-risk individuals, which is unjust towards low-risk individuals. This is not very convincing, however, since everybody will have to pay the higher premiums such tolerance would result in, including the high-risk individuals. Low-risk individuals are therefore not discriminated against in this respect.

To gain further support against regulation, one has to leave purely actuarial concerns and instead refer to more general intuitions of justice. For instance, there is the claim that the cost of compensating genetically high-risk individuals should be borne by all those who are more fortunate and better off, and not just by those who have chosen to invest in private personal insurance. This does not speak directly in favour of absence of regulation, however. Instead, it is an argument for generally subsidised compensation from society, where people pay according to capacity and receive according to need.

The line of reasoning above shows, perhaps not surprisingly, that the actuarial ideal is best seen as internal to the business of private insurance – not as a general principle of justice. Moreover, as shown by its use within insurance, it is just one consideration of many that can be weighed against one another in case of conflict with, for example, economic factors. Because of this, the actuarial ideal leaves plenty of room for people to refrain from genetic testing or from sharing information from such tests in connection with applications for private insurance.

If, instead, actuarial fairness were interpreted as a *strict* ideal that insurance companies *should* do their best to comply with, the actual procedures of risk assessment followed by insurance companies would have to undergo rather far-reaching revision. It seems quite difficult to predict what the result of such revision would be for the business of private insurance, as well as society as a whole. Consequently, it is even more difficult to describe what a strict ideal of actuarial fairness would have to say about genetic testing in connection with insurance.

7.5.3.2 Libertarianism   Even if ideals of actuarial fairness will not do the job, there are *basic* ideas of justice that appear to support the right of insurance companies both to ask for information from old tests and to demand that new tests be made, that is, that support absence of regulation. These are the *libertarian* theories of justice, of which the most famous is Robert Nozick's theory of entitlement.[35] Libertarian theories are at one in endorsing a strong kind of free market system without taxation and (stricter) regulation. Our criticism will extend in part to all these libertarian theories when it comes to criticising the libertarian conclusions they allegedly reach, but we will concentrate most of our criticism on Nozick's particular theory.

A short recapitulation of Nozick's theory of justice is in order. The theory's basic assumption is that we have certain absolute rights, first and foremost to our body and to property acquired justly.[36] By virtue of this, no one may prevent an individual from using his body and justly acquired property in the way he himself sees fit, as long as this person does not violate the same rights of anyone else (I may destroy my justly acquired car if I want to do so, but not by driving it through your porch). If all property is justly acquired, every voluntary transaction that does not violate anyone's rights will result in a just distribution, no matter what the pattern of distribution looks like. 'A distribution is just if it arises from another just distribution by legitimate means' (1974, p. 151) is Nozick's concise statement of this idea.

According to libertarianism, each individual is free to choose the terms he himself wants when engaging in a transaction with property to which he is entitled, just as he is free to accept or reject the terms of the other party to the transaction. This implies that insurance companies may demand information about the insurance applicant's genetic constitution as a term of an insurance contract, if they choose to do so. If the insured person deliberately withholds such information, the insurance company has the right to compensation from the insured person, and the state has a duty to force the insured party to pay compensation. Justice for the insured party is constituted by the fact that he could have rejected the

---

[35] Other theories will support the same conclusions in this respect, e.g. Gauthier and his theory of morals by agreement (1986). However, we shall here take it for granted that Gauthier's theory has these implications (see instead Gauthier, 1986; or Kymlicka, 1990, p. 132 ff.; or Holtug, 1999, p. 288).

[36] Because of past injustices there probably is no property today which has been justly acquired, which makes Nozick's theory difficult to realise.

contract and chosen not to engage in the transaction, if he found the terms unacceptable. The reasoning here is thus similar to that supported by Mill's ideal of respect for autonomy (see section 7.3.2 above).

The major problem with libertarianism is that it has normatively unacceptable consequences, which is clear in this case. According to libertarianism, taxation is a violation of the right to property, even if the income from taxation saves lives or prevents extensive suffering (Kymlicka, 1990, pp. 96 f.). People in dire straits instead have to rely on the voluntary beneficence of others. If private personal insurance companies demand genetic information and use this to differentiate premiums, which they most certainly will do if they are allowed to, those suffering from genetically caused diseases may be left totally without means to provide for the most basic material necessities for survival. This consequence should be enough to make most people reject libertarianism.

The basis of libertarianism, however, seems sound. It is an appealing thought that each individual should be the sovereign owner of his own body with its attributes and capacities, and that he should be allowed to use this as he himself chooses, as long as he respects the rights of others. Perhaps, then, the above-mentioned consequences are the price we have to pay in order to uphold this fine ideal of personal liberty. However, these consequences follow only if Nozick's further claim, that this thesis of self-ownership implies the absolute right to external property justly acquired, is accepted. Property, according to Nozick, can be justly acquired either through original acquisition of previously un-owned nature, or through voluntary transactions between autonomous individuals. We have the right to acquire parts of the external world, as long as they have not been previously acquired and we leave 'enough and as good' parts to others (Nozick, 1974, p. 202).[37] This last condition on legitimate original acquisition has been called 'Locke's proviso'[38] and has been the subject of much debate. The outcome of the debate shows that the basis of Nozick's theory does not imply a general resistance to taxation or regulation of the market as obviously as he thought.

Hillel Steiner (1997) has argued that a reasonable interpretation of the basis of libertarianism leads to non-libertarian conclusions. According to Steiner, each individual, on the basis of his right to use his body and talents to achieve prosperity, has an original justified claim of access to

[37] How the acquisition should be made in order to be legitimate is unclear. Do I have to 'mix labour' with that which I acquire (which seems to have been the position of Locke)? In that case what exactly do I acquire (if I use part of a tree to make a chair, do I acquire the whole tree, the parts I am using or just the product)? Is it enough to fence a thing in or 'claim' it in order to acquire it?

[38] From Locke, who originally formulated this, 1689.

an *equal* part of (the value of) natural resources. If natural resources have already been acquired by earlier generations, then these generations have a duty to share the (value of) natural resources with new individuals. Steiner continues his argument by claiming that if everyone has such an equal right to natural resources, then we also share an obligation to carry the costs of whims of nature. The genes of an individual are a result of such whims of nature.[39] This seems to favour an obligation to compensate those who suffer adverse consequences as a result of their genes. It is an issue of appropriateness how this compensation should be implemented – through a regulation that limits insurance companies' rights to use genetic information, or via a social insurance system. It is important to notice that the compensation cannot be left to voluntary beneficence, since there is a *right* to compensation if Steiner is correct.

Further perspectives can be brought to bear on the idea that Nozick is not entitled to deduce the conclusions he does. Nozick claims that Locke's proviso is compatible with individuals acquiring a larger part of natural resources than the part each would have acquired by equal distribution. On the other hand, Nozick claims that the acquisition of a part of natural resources that makes others worse off materially than they would have been had that part of nature never been acquired is illegitimate. This interpretation of Locke's proviso has been widely criticised. The background to the criticism is that Nozick defends the principle of self-ownership with reference to the ideal – vital to all forms of liberal ideals – that each individual's right to live his life according to his own ideas of what is valuable should be respected (Nozick, 1974, p. 50).

This raises the question as to why Nozick emphasises making others worse off materially and not worse off in terms of their ability to lead the life they themselves as individuals find valuable (Cohen, 1986). If the ability to lead the life the individual himself finds valuable is the basic tenet underlying Nozick's theory, why is there according to him no obligation to support those who cannot do this without the help of others (Holtug, 1999, p. 289)? Many of those suffering from genetically caused diseases obviously belong to this group, and this may imply far-reaching obligations to help these people. For instance, Kymlicka (1990, p. 113) has argued that if the possibility of leading a life that the individual values determines the relevance of worsening aspects of his life, the resulting demands for redistribution of resources may be extensive.

---

[39] To an increasing extent, this can be questioned. Preimplantation and prenatal genetic diagnoses make it possible for parents to choose the genetic make-up of their children. The responsibility for the consequences of that make-up could then be claimed to belong to the parents, thus making them the party that should provide compensation, according to Steiner.

7.5.4   *Justice: a compromise*

Even if libertarianism is hard to defend generally, it may be defendable partially. A dominating opinion in Western societies is that market transactions are an appropriate and efficient method of distribution for a wide variety of goods. Very few people are morally indignant at the fact that, for example, golf equipment and Beatles records are distributed by supply and demand. Most people lead good lives without the right to support for the purchase of such dispensable commodities. On the contrary, most people think that a right to receive support is limited to certain goods that are of vital concern to people's welfare, such as health care, education and food. These vital goods should be accessible to all, and, if necessary, we are justified in implementing, or maybe even obliged to implement, some mechanism of redistribution to provide these goods to those unable to purchase them on the market.

Private personal insurance is increasingly becoming a vital good of this type, due to the dismantling of social insurance that guarantees all citizens access to health care and provision in case of disease. The social role of insurance companies is consequently changing. This has led some to claim that insurance companies have obligations other than those of profit-maximising business in general – obligations of a social kind (Chadwick and Ngwena, 1995, p. 122). The fact that access to private personal insurance is increasingly becoming necessary for the security and welfare of the individual makes it reasonable to apply stricter regulations to personal insurance than to goods such as golf equipment and Beatles records. Such, at least, is the general idea.

This is an argument for justice of a communitarian kind, and can be supported with reference to considerations of principle. The most obvious reference here is to Walzer and his *magnum opus* on justice: *Spheres of Justice: A Defence of Pluralism and Equality*, 1983.

Walzer's point of departure is that a society, or, more generally, a culture, has shared, important values and ways of seeing social relations. Different societies regard different things as goods, depending on these values (pp. 8 f.). The term 'goods' has a broad meaning and should be understood as everything positively valued and distributed according to societal norms, including public offices and social relations. Whether a thing is a good or not is partially determined by the function that this thing fulfils in people's relations, or its *role*. Money is an example: it is of value in our society because it functions as a means of exchanging commodities and services. Some things are valued in several different cultures, but often to different degrees and for different reasons. For instance, cattle are considered valuable as food in one culture, while another culture values them for their religious significance.

These examples illustrate the fact that different goods have different *social meanings*. This term refers to the common evaluation and understanding of a certain thing in a certain society. The following claim is crucial to an understanding of Walzer's theory of justice: the principle of distribution that should be applied to a certain good is determined by or is a part of the social meaning of this good (p. 20). For Western societies of the type that are of concern here, Walzer discerns three basic principles of distribution (pp. 21 ff.): the principle of desert, the principle of need (resembling the principles of equality discussed above) and free exchange (resembling the libertarian principle discussed above). For instance, it is part of the social meaning of punishment in Western societies that it should be distributed according to guilt (negative desert), while favoured positions, such as jobs, should be allotted to the person with the greatest merit (positive desert), and health care should be distributed according to need. Non-vital material commodities, however, are to be distributed on the basis of free exchange. That all this has a banal ring is because we have a common understanding of the social meanings of these goods, which also tell us how they should be distributed.

Following this, a just society is a society of complex equality, as opposed to simple equality (where everyone has the same amount of every good). Complex equality means absence of dominance (p. 16), which means that we should not be allowed to use one type of good to acquire goods that have another social meaning. In our society, the commonly agreed injustice of being able to use money in order to avoid punishment is an obvious example. Walzer expresses this thought by saying that different goods demarcate different spheres, and that justice prevails when spheres do not impose on one another.

With this theory of justice as our point of departure the question thus becomes: what is the social meaning of personal insurance? Attempts have been made to answer this question in the spirit of Walzer, but this has proved to be a somewhat difficult task (Lemmens, 1999). This difficulty is partly due to the fact that the social meaning of a good is to some extent determined by its relation to other goods. The task is further complicated by the historical dynamics, according to which the social meaning of some goods gradually changes. That is, a type of good which belongs in one sphere and to which one type of distributive ideal is applicable, may, due to social change, move into another sphere, thereby making other distributive ideals more appropriate for this type of good. This is what seems to be happening with personal insurance.

Traditionally, at least, private personal insurance has been considered as a good among others to be exchanged on a free market according to supply and demand: it is bought to satisfy 'private desires of certainty' (Lemmens, 1999, p. 34). However, since we are in a situation where public social insurance systems are weakened, private personal insurance has a tendency to become more vital to guarantee basic welfare. Private personal insurance is developing into a necessary means of compensating for loss of income or providing for health care in the event of disease and of compensating for loss of income in case of the premature death of family providers.

Walzer argues that health care is a typical example of a good that should be distributed according to need (pp. 86 ff.). No one in our society should have to be left without access to it. The principles of the market should therefore not interfere with this sphere. This does not imply that private personal insurance should be banned, but if health care should be distributed according to need, it should be accessible to the individual regardless of his success in the competitive market.

The obligations of insurance companies must therefore be judged taking into account the rest of society. In the present day European Union countries, the major part of health care is funded by taxes (Nys *et al.*, 1993) and is distributed according to some vaguely formulated criterion of need (e.g. SOU 1995:5, p. 22). This situation is changing (see chapter 4). If health care should be distributed according to need, the following argument seems reasonable from a 'Walzerian' point of view: the obligation of insurance companies to provide everybody with personal health insurance is in proportion to the absence of social insurance systems. Someone has to see to it that the needy get the care they are entitled to, and if the state does not provide for this redistribution, insurance companies must do so. For this to be accomplished, some sort of rather strict regulation is probably necessary.

We have seen, however, that it is a risky business to leave this responsibility to private insurance, because of the problem of adverse selection (see chapter 5, section 5.4). For Walzer, it makes no difference in itself how we regulate insurance companies' access to and use of genetic information. The important thing, according to his theory in this regard, is that no one is left without the goods that are part of 'the sphere of Security and Welfare', which should be distributed according to need. Health care, education and commodities such as food and housing belong to this sphere. If we are to allow private personal insurance, it must not threaten anyone's access to these goods. But such a threat is exactly the one posed by the problem of adverse selection. For this reason, the suggestion that insurance companies should be forced to provide health insurance according to need does not seem to be a sustainable solution. The remaining solution, then, is to reverse the weakening of social security systems. Walzer's conclusion in this regard, then, is similar to those implied by the principles of equality and the principle of desert.

7.5.5   Justice: summary

The principles and theories of justice investigated here seem to lead to different conclusions regarding the appropriateness of regulation. Prima facie, the principle of desert, according to which no one should suffer adverse consequences on account of things for which he is not responsible, seems to support total regulation. Three principles of equality (the difference principle, the priority principle and the principle of need) seem to support the same conclusion. All these principles defend a far-reaching equality in the distribution of the resources of society. On closer scrutiny the prima facie impression fades away, and it becomes clear that the principles do not speak directly for or against any kind of regulation. They all lead to the conclusion that (if possible) no one should be without basic goods because of increased susceptibility to disease due to genetic constitution. These principles in themselves, however, do not imply how this should be achieved.

Other theories of justice, such as libertarianism and actuarial fairness, seem to speak straightforwardly in favour of an absence of regulation. Actuarial fairness says that no one should have to pay a larger premium than is justified by the known risk he represents. This idea does not have much plausibility as a basic and strict principle of justice, however. What could be claimed is that it is unjust that costs for high-risk individuals should be carried by all those who are more fortunate, not just those who have invested in private insurance. This is an argument in favour of collectively financed insurance for these individuals. Nozick's brand of libertarianism supports absence of regulation. While this theory of justice has what seem to be implausible normative implications, on closer examination, however, it is not obvious that it has such implication at all.

Walzer's theory of justice, which can be described as a compromise between libertarian and egalitarian theories of justice, has also been examined. This theory answers the question of the rights and duties of insurance companies by referring to the social meaning of personal insurance. It favours the same practical conclusions as the theories of equality: some basic goods, such as health care and a decent standard of living, should, in an affluent society such as ours, be granted to everyone.

7.6   Conclusion

This chapter has investigated four ethical perspectives that have been used to argue for and against the right of insurance companies to genetic information: considerations of consequence, autonomy, privacy and justice respectively. The point of departure has been to assume the absence of regulation, in order to examine whether there exist ethical arguments that support a departure from this situation in favour of some sort of regulation.

Consequentialist arguments do not speak unequivocally in favour of any type of regulation, since all kinds of regulation, including the absence of regulation, may reasonably be seen to lead to serious negative consequences, at least given the ongoing dismantling of collective social insurance systems. Some ideals of autonomy (those of Mill) are compatible with absence of regulation, while others (self-realisation) seem to support some sort of regulation. Genetic privacy can be used to argue in favour of total regulation. Such regulation may not be as effective a means of protecting privacy as is intended. Privacy can be protected, to some extent at least, by generous social insurance, which can also reduce the worry about genetic information. Total regulation may be counterproductive in this regard. Considerations of justice do not speak unequivocally in favour of regulation either. Some principles or ideals of justice (actuarial fairness and libertarianism) seem to favour the absence of regulation. However, on closer examination, these ideals are hard to defend. The other theories of justice (the principle of desert, the principles of equality and Walzer's theory) imply that individuals should be compensated for genetic burdens as far as is possible, but whether this should be done by private personal insurance or by collective social insurance is left an open question by these theories.

There is no certain answer to be found in this ethical analysis of the question of how insurance companies' access to genetic information should be regulated. The different considerations examined point in different directions regarding their conclusions on the matter. The reasonable ethical arguments discussed seem to be unanimous on one point, however: the basic institutions of society should be designed in such a way that no one has to suffer excessive burdens due to his genetic constitution. How this should be achieved is the subject of the next and concluding chapter.

Part IV

Evaluation

8   Conclusions and policy implications

8.1   Introduction

We have now reached the end of the road in our review of the questions that arise as a consequence of the partial dismantling of the traditional social insurance systems and of the simultaneous advances of genetic science, along with the potential usefulness of genetic insights for the insurance industry. The purpose of this chapter is to provide a background to the regulation in force in many countries constraining the possibilities of using genetic insights for the purpose of insurance (section 8.2), to summarise the arguments for and against this regulation (section 8.3), and, importantly, to discuss whether regulation really serves its purpose, or if other action is needed to resolve the emerging and potential problems caused by the above confluence of events (section 8.4).

Initially, however, it is important to provide a reminder of a central starting point for our work. Insurance to provide protection against income shortfalls during illness, in the event of premature death, and during old age, in all cases up to a level at which reasonable comfort can be assured, provides a utility of vital importance to the individual's welfare.[1] There are strong reasons, both economic and ethical, in favour of the view that everyone should be assured access to such a utility. Our work would lose much of its justification if this starting point were invalid.

Our approach is forward looking; in this respect it differs from the static views that characterise part of the literature on which our study is based. The reform of social insurance systems and the expansion of

---

[1] In principle, such assurance of income could be based on private savings, particularly for high income groups. In practice, however, a majority of the population is dependent on insurance, private or public, to achieve these ends. This is especially true for income assurance and provision of livelihood in the event of illness and premature death given the unpredictability of both, and the large financial requirements to which they may give rise. But insurance solutions are also quite important, for providing income during old age. Since it is not possible to predict an individual's remaining length of life, it would be difficult to substitute straightforward private savings for actuarially based pension schemes.

the genetic insights are still at an early stage. The consequences of the developments that have hitherto taken place will be unremarkable, but we expect further and more far-reaching impacts from the changes to come. Our analysis seeks to extend the recent trends into the future, to illuminate their ultimate consequences. This research strategy is admittedly risky but, in our view, appropriate.

8.2   Reduced scope of social insurance and genetic progress, and restrained access to genetic insights for the purpose of insurance

Since the early 1990s the extensive systems of collective and obligatory social insurance in Europe and north America have been subjected to a partial dismantling. This dismantling has included (i) more restrictive criteria entitling health and invalidity benefits, and pension benefits before the statutory pension age; (ii) a more careful control of individual insurance claims before payments are made; (iii) widened deductibles; (iv) declining compensation levels in real terms brought about by an unwillingness to index payments to rising incomes and inflation; and (v) an increasing tendency to shift part of the responsibility for employees' sickness and pension benefits to the employers. As was discussed in chapter 4, several factors have triggered these changes. There is, first, an ideological reorientation, with increasing awareness of the inherent deficiencies of the collective systems and a greater belief in the ability of freely functioning markets efficiently to address emerging economic and social problems in rich societies. Second, there is the increased difficulty in generating the fiscal revenue needed to finance the swelling social insurance bill.

It is not very surprising that the partial dismantling of the social insurance system has led to an expanding demand for individual sickness and premature death insurance and for pension policies. This, in turn, has prompted a parallel increase in the supply of such goods from private insurance companies that operate in competitive markets. Private insurance is becoming an increasingly important supplement to social insurance and a good of growing significance in ensuring basic welfare. The authorities in many countries have encouraged such tendencies to privatisation and individualisation.

There is no need for individual risk assessments in collective and obligatory social insurance systems. Such assessments acquire critical importance, however, when the insurance policies are issued to individuals by private, profit maximising, insurance companies. Efficiency and profitability in the insurance business requires that premiums are set on actuarial grounds, that is, that the premium paid for each individual risk is adjusted to the size of that risk in each case (chapter 3).

The partial dismantling of social insurance has occurred in parallel with the developments in genetic science. In the course of the 1990s it has become possible to employ genetic insights for identifying individuals who carry an increased risk of incurring one or more of a group of serious hereditary diseases with a very high cost of treatment and/or likelihood of premature death. Differing views currently prevail about the future prospects of genetic science as a tool for risk assessments. A cautious scenario holds that genetic testing will not be able to predict increased individual likelihoods for a majority of the most common diseases. A bolder scenario envisages far greater future prospects for using genetic insights in the determination of the risk of incurring a broad array of illnesses. The bold scenario also posits that progress in genetic science is contributing to the development of related biochemical tests which can come to be used to predict likelihoods of illness and longevity (chapter 2). It is already possible to draw on genetic insights for assessing the risks represented by individuals who seek insurance. The importance of such insights is bound to rise, if for no other reason than genetic testing for diagnostic and predictive medical purposes will cover widening population groups. As genetic tests become increasingly common, their costs are likely to fall, making them more attractive as tools for the differentiation of insurance premiums, while at the same time an expanding population group will possess information about the extent of its genetic health risks. The insurance companies' incentives to access such information, so as to limit the prevalence of asymmetric information and adverse selection, will therefore be enhanced.

These prospects are juxtaposed against the fact that already, at the turn of the twentieth century, the governments of a number of the rich market economies around the north Atlantic had regulated insurance companies' access to genetic information. The proclaimed reasons for these restrictions comprised a desire to implement a certain degree of redistributive solidarity between the insured individuals, protection of their privacy and autonomy, and, finally, a wish to avoid situations where individuals representing high risks experience difficulties in finding cover for those risks, or are refused insurance altogether (chapter 3). The restrictive regulation of insurance companies' access to genetic information has created a dilemma. The need of instruments for individual risk assessments has risen because of the current developments in personal insurance. At the same time, the use of an emerging instrument of great potential importance for such assessments has been, by and large, forbidden.

8.3   Ethical aspects and practical consequences

We summarise in the following paragraphs the ethical arguments that can be adduced for and against the existing restraints on insurance companies' access to genetic information (section 8.3.1), and the practical consequences that will follow from these restraints (section 8.3.2). This material then constitutes the starting point for exploring whether the regulation is likely to attain its purported goals (section 8.4).

8.3.1   Ethical aspects

As should be clear from our discussions in chapter 7, the existing restrictions on insurance companies' access to genetic information have been motivated by reference to a set of ethical considerations. The arguments in favour of restrictive regulation appear to be strongly anchored in international research in the field of ethics.

An absolute right of insurance firms to ask for information from already existing genetic tests, and, furthermore, to ask that new tests be undertaken, as a condition for underwriting policy, arouses a number of ethical problems. These can be divided into at least three categories.

A first category of ethical problems arises from the negative welfare consequences that can hit individuals in consequence of the insurance companies' demand. One example is the individual's right to remain ignorant about possible deficiencies in his genetic constitution. From a medical point of view there may be clear advantages to be aware of such deficiencies, for then the individual has a chance to undergo prophylactic treatment, or to adjust his behaviour and lifestyle so as to avoid or at least reduce the negative consequences of his genetic make-up. However, full awareness of genetic shortcomings can result in anxiety or depression, with ensuing adverse psychological or social consequences. Furthermore, the individual may not be able to obtain insurance, either for the specific genetic risks or at all, if the negative results from genetic testing have to be handed over to the insurer. Clearly, ignorance about his genetic constitution may be preferred by the individual in some cases, and this preference provides one argument in favour of restrictions on insurance companies' access to genetic information.

A second category of problems relates to the individual's basic rights to autonomy and privacy. It is a common view that autonomy is a precondition to self-fulfilment. We showed (chapter 7) that the insurance companies' access to genetic information could reduce the scope for self-fulfilment in some circumstances. The right to privacy, that is, a private sphere to which no one else can demand access, is of great importance to most people. The genetic constitution is one of the most intimate attributes of the individual. Some aspects of this attribute, such as height or physical strength, cannot be hidden, but many others will be revealed only through genetic tests. Outsiders' claims to share such insights will be regarded by many as an infringement of privacy. This, then, is another argument in favour of restricting insurance companies' access to genetic information.

The third and probably most important category of problems relates to equality and justice. Ethical analyses of what is required to provide equal opportunities to all citizens often distinguish between three levels, ranked by ever greater aims for equality (Buchanan *et al.*, 2000, p. 65). (i) A fundamental requirement of equality and justice is the elimination of any existing legal grounds for discrimination. (ii) At the next level, equality requires that informal discrimination, based for instance on culture or religion, and related to race, gender and religion among others, be eradicated. (iii) The third level is the most far-reaching: its proponents argue, additionally, for efforts to eliminate handicaps in whatever field, for example social or medical, following from bad luck for which the individual cannot be made responsible. Such handicaps may obviously arise from genetic deficiencies. In order to cover their damage costs, private, profit-maximising insurance companies with free access to genetic information will, as a matter of course, either limit the insurance cover, or charge higher premiums to individuals who suffer from such deficiencies and therefore represent high insurance risks. To avoid such an outcome, proponents of this third level of equality and justice will argue against insurance companies' use of genetic information for premium determination.

This view of justice is selectively applied in the rich north Atlantic countries, for instance as an argument in favour of support for the physically handicapped, or for basic schooling for all children. At the same time, it is important to point out that a general requirement that public authorities should eliminate *all* existing inequalities due to handicaps caused by circumstances beyond the handicapped individuals' control would involve quite radical changes of the societies under review, and a conflict with the goal of economic efficiency. One can even question whether the general application of such a policy of justice is at all compatible with a market-oriented economic system.

The importance of the above ethical arguments must not be underestimated. At the same time, we must recall the ethical arguments brought up in chapter 7, which point in an opposite policy direction. The justice and equality considerations discussed above can be juxtaposed against actuarial justice, according to which no one should pay more for his insurance than the cost of the risk that he imposes on the insurance company. Other arguments in favour of the insurance companies' use of genetic information have also been brought up in the ethical debate. Thus, it has been pointed out that insurance is a voluntary contract and that sensitive individuals can avoid an infringement of their privacy following from disclosure of their genetic make-up simply by refraining from taking out insurance. Questions have also been raised as to why restrictions are directed specifically towards genetic information, while other medical information can be freely used to differentiate insurance premiums. Proposals for new legislation in Norway (see chapter 3, section 3.4.3) indicate that this point of view is gaining ground.

8.3.2   *Practical consequences*

Serious concerns have been widely voiced that restrictions and prohibitions on the use of genetic information could undermine private insurance activities in competitive markets, with dire consequences for society as a whole. A basic purpose of the efforts to individualise and privatise social insurance in the course of the 1990s has been to improve the efficiency in production and distribution of personal insurance products. The creation and maintenance of an unrestrained competitive market is a necessary precondition for cost reduction and efficiency. The operation of such a market makes it possible for the individual to equalise the marginal cost and marginal utility of insurance, and so to avoid inadequate or excessive insurance protection. A freely operating competitive market is therefore a prerequisite for success in maximising the utility derived by society from the resources expended on insurance to protect against illness and premature death, and to provide pensions during old age.

8.3.2.1 Partial regulation   Partial regulation prevents insurance companies from asking for new genetic tests to be undertaken as a precondition for obtaining insurance. But it allows them access to existing genetic tests. The negative practical consequences of such regulation will be limited but not insignificant. The constraint on insurance companies' freedom to obtain relevant information about the insured risk reduces the ability to charge premiums that correspond to the actual risk in each individual case. This, in turn, will create a likelihood that the insurance policies that are taken out will in many cases be either inadequate or excessive. On the other hand, since the buyers of insurance are not permitted to withhold existing genetic information from the insurance company under partial regulation, there is little likelihood of adverse selection, the most serious threat to the insurance industry in this context. At the same time, the significance of partial regulation will be continuously diluted as genetic tests become increasingly common.

8.3.2.2 Total regulation   The application of total regulation which prevents insurance companies not only from asking for new genetic tests but also from sharing the results of existing tests, is likely to have serious economic consequences for the insurance industry. Total regulation will lead to asymmetric information and an ensuing adverse selection. This will develop into an ever more serious handicap to the insurers, as genetic testing becomes increasingly common (the progress of genetic science and technology will determine the ultimate seriousness of the handicap). The insurers' problems will be accentuated by an intensification of international trade in insurance (chapter 5), permitting individuals who represent low genetic risks to buy polices at low premiums from suppliers outside the regulation's reach. Ultimately, only the individuals representing high genetic risks will insure themselves in countries where total regulation is applied. The premiums must gradually be raised in those countries, in parallel with rising average damage payments. In an extreme case, the premiums will rise to levels where those representing the highest risks will either lose interest in signing policies, or will not be able to afford them, and the market for personal insurance will ultimately dry up. Then, if not before, it will be evident that total regulation, established for the purpose of protecting individuals' autonomy and privacy, and to guarantee insurance protection to those with an inopportune genetic make-up, has failed to serve its purpose.

The fears and complications expressed above can possibly be seen as overly alarmist against the background of empirical investigations which claim to demonstrate that the adverse selection problems are not that serious to the insurance industry (Smith *et al.*, 1999, p. 59). But empirical observations can only detect phenomena that have already occurred. And in our view, the necessary time perspective is insufficiently taken into account in the studies cited by Smith *et al.* With the dynamic development of genetic science, we expect (chapter 2) that genetic tests undertaken primarily on medical grounds will become very common in the next one to two decades. Within the foreseeable future, therefore, a majority of the population will have been genetically tested, and those with a defective genetic make-up will have important insights into the risk of serious illness or premature death to which they are subject. If domestic insurance companies are prevented from access to this information, while at the same time it is readily available to insurers operating beyond the reach of regulation, it would be hard to deny the existence of a potentially serious adverse selection problem.

We noted in chapter 3 that some countries have chosen to apply total regulation only in cases where the insured sums exceed a limit value. Such a limitation in the application of total regulation reduces the total amount of risks that can be insured on the basis of asymmetric information, and the problem of adverse selection is correspondingly reduced. But since limit values have been set quite high in most cases, the problem of adverse selection nevertheless remains serious.

8.4   Future policy implications

Current developments in the field that is the focus of our study result in a dilemma of increasing severity. The demand for private insurance to cover the hazards of sickness and premature death, and to secure pension payments during old age, is expanding briskly in consequence of the partial dismantling of social insurance, and the satisfaction of this demand is acquiring an increasing significance for welfare provision. The progress of genetic knowledge provides improving means of individual risk assessments when such insurance policies are signed. Freedom of access for insurance companies to genetic information for the purpose of premium differentiation or of determining the extent of insurance cover infringes the insurance clients' autonomy and privacy, and, more importantly, threatens to leave the groups representing high genetic risks entirely or partially without private insurance cover. Many rich market economies have chosen to avoid this problem by constraining the insurance industry's access to genetic information. It is clear, however, that the policy-makers who have introduced such regulation have not undertaken any careful analysis of its longer-term consequences.

8.4.1   Partial regulation

Our analysis shows that the negative economic consequences of partial regulation for the insurance industry are limited. They are also temporary, and will lose much of their significance once a majority of the population has undergone genetic testing. Nevertheless, there is a need for society to make a conscious trade-off between these consequences and the ethical arguments discussed above that point in favour of such regulation. In our view, it is hard to direct serious criticism against partial regulation in a trade-off of this kind.

8.4.2   Total regulation

At the same time our analyses demonstrate that the total regulation introduced in a number of countries will lead to increasing problems for the insurance industry, with gradually rising premiums on account of accentuated adverse selection, ultimately resulting in a collapse of the entire market for personal insurance. On this account, total regulation will clearly not accomplish its purported ethical objectives. This statement holds especially true if our bold scenario with regard to the potential of genetic science proves realistic. *In our view, therefore, total regulation should be abrogated.* We have demonstrated (chapter 6) that this regulation is not anchored in any uniform system of legal principles concerning discrimination in private activities. To our knowledge, no such system is in existence. A repeal of total regulation, therefore, does not conflict with any basic legal principles.

Our policy proposal would trigger the emergence of three latent problems. (i) Individuals who possess genetic information about themselves can fail to obtain adequate insurance cover if they decide against releasing such information to the insurance company. The same applies to individuals who do share such information with the insurance company, where it could point to a very high insurance risk. (ii) Individuals who have not yet undergone genetic testing could decide against such testing even when it is strongly desirable, on medical grounds for example, for fear that they may be refused insurance. The potential medical benefits of genetics would be stifled as a result. The significance of both problems hinges on the character of the insurance products under review. Serious issues will arise only when insurance is of vital importance to the individual's basic welfare. (iii) There is furthermore the problem of infringement of the autonomy and privacy of an individual who possesses genetic information about himself, if he wishes to buy insurance and has no alternative to releasing that information to the insurance company. This, too, becomes a serious problem only when the insurance product is of vital importance to his welfare; for if it is not, the infringement can be avoided without undue consequences by refraining from taking out insurance.

The thrust of our argument, therefore, is that the seriousness of the problem is basically determined by the importance for the individual's basic welfare of sickness, premature death and pension insurance. This, in turn, depends on the extent of existing social insurance systems. One of the starting points for our analysis was that the reformed social insurance system no longer provides an adequate protection, and that this protection will be even more depleted by the continued process of dismantling. Our starting point is vindicated by the emergence of the regulation of genetic information. If social insurance arrangements had continued to provide adequate protection, and private insurance had remained a mere 'luxury good', then regulation would have been unnecessary.

We deem that the consequences of repealing the regulation of genetic information for the purpose of insurance are not acceptable in rich welfare societies. Further measures must therefore be employed to neutralise the problems that will emerge when regulation ends. The most appropriate way of preventing infringements of the individual's autonomy and privacy, and the threat that insurance will not be offered at all, would be to reduce individual dependence on private personal insurance.[2]

The obvious means of achieving this would be by raising the compensation levels in social insurance.[3] In a situation where each individual was guaranteed compensation from the public system in the event of sickness or premature death and during old age, at a level that corresponds to what the public authorities assess as a minimum necessary for basic welfare maintenance, the inability to obtain private insurance would not be a serious social problem. Neither would the demand of insurance companies to have access to the results of existing genetic tests constitute a serious threat to an individual's autonomy and privacy. However, an increase in social insurance compensation levels would involve a halt to the partial dismantling of social insurance, discussed in chapter 4. Public involvements in broad welfare provisions would again be expanded. The improvement of individual welfare protection would revive the economic inefficiencies and other problems that caused the partial dismantling of wide public security nets in the first place.

A reduction of individual dependence on private personal insurance could obviously also be achieved through less radical means. Those who fail to obtain adequate private insurance, either because they cannot afford the premiums they are charged, or because they are refused such insurance protection altogether in the private market, could be offered the option to buy such protection from a publicly subsidised high-risk pool (Brom, 1991, p. 146), whose maximum compensation level would correspond to what the public authorities consider to be necessary to assure basic welfare. In this case too, the improvement in the individual's basic protection would take the form of a publicly financed expansion of social insurance (interpreted broadly), and would probably involve

---

[2] Hertzman, 1996, p. 197, states that 'public authorities must organize insurance in all fields where political goals stipulate distributional arrangements that differ from those which can be accomplished through private arrangements'.

[3] This line of thought is evident in Brom, 1991, p. 146, even though Brom's thinking has apparently been influenced by existing health care arrangements in the United States.

reduced economic efficiency. But since this insurance protection would be acquired on a voluntary basis, and would have to be paid for in part by the individuals themselves, one can argue that their own preferences would be reflected in some measure, and hence, the efficiency losses would be smaller compared with what would follow from a general increase in social insurance compensation levels. From the point of view of economic efficiency, therefore, this more selective arrangement appears to be preferable.

However, difficult trade-offs are bound to arise in the selection of individuals with the right to use the high-risk pool. Since the main purpose of the pool is to reduce the effects that follow from the insurers' freedom to use genetic information, one can argue that access to the pool should be limited to those who fail to get adequate insurance on account of genetic circumstances. Defining the term 'genetic circumstances' is not a simple matter, however. Furthermore, limitation to such a criterion could be criticised as unjust on the same grounds as the regulation of insurance companies' access to genetic information (chapters 3 and 7). Why should the pool's support be limited to those whose problems arise solely from genetic causes? Should not individuals whose difficulty in obtaining insurance is caused by general health problems also be allowed to avail themselves of the pool's subsidised insurance facilities?

'Failure to get adequate insurance' gives rise to further ambiguities in the identification of the group that should be supported. 'Failure' clearly applies to individuals who are refused insurance in the private market altogether. But what is less clear is how the group which does not face straightforward refusal, but which is asked to pay exorbitant premiums for the insurance service, or which is offered policies with severely restricted cover, should be classified. Should the group comprise only those individuals who cannot reasonably afford the high charges, or also those who conceivably could, but choose not to because of the high cost? What about those who have bought insurance despite its high price but are consequently unable to afford other welfare necessities? And how should the line be drawn between cover restrictions that warrant public support and those that do not? A further complication is bound to arise in determining the size of the subsidies.

We conclude that on economic efficiency grounds a state-supported high-risk pool is preferable to a general increase in social insurance compensation levels. But at the same time it is clear that a high-risk pool carries transaction costs that are likely to be much higher than a general restoration of compensation levels. It is unclear to us which of the two approaches would generally be preferable on balance, and it is possible that some combination of the two would prove to be a better solution. What is indubitable is that in both cases expanded basic insurance protection builds on public financing and so involves a reconstruction, in a broad sense, of social insurance. Some of the desired economic efficiency gains which initially prompted the partial dismantling of the public system are likely to be lost from these adjustments. The real gain will be in the form of greater satisfaction of ethical goals such as equality and justice, and an ensuing improvement in welfare levels for losers in the privatisation and commercialisation of social insurance and of the simultaneous progress in genetic science.

8.4.3   A final consideration

A general conclusion emerging from the analyses contained in this book is that both the partial dismantling of the social insurance systems and the prohibitions against the use of genetic information in the insurance field have been initiated without a proper analysis of the consequences. Our book presents such an analysis, and points out that the two policy efforts in combination do not fulfil the purported objectives and therefore need to be modified. We have shown that the prohibition against the use of results from existing genetic tests is not tenable in the longer run. And we deem that the ethical problems likely to affect a group of individuals, as increasingly sophisticated genetic tests are taken up by the insurance industry, are best handled through an expanded public commitment to assure the incomes of genetically disadvantaged groups in connection with illness or premature death and during old age. Our plea for a re-expansion of collective social insurance in some form involves a clear dilemma. Such an expansion might well revive some of the problems that originally prompted the decision to implement a partial dismantling of the social insurance system.

Bibliography

International legal instruments

United Nations

Conventions
International Convention on the Elimination of All Forms of Racial Discrimination (1965)
International Covenant on Civil and Political Rights (1966)

Declarations
UNESCO, Universal Declaration on the Human Genome and Human Rights, 11 November 1997

European Community

Treaties
Treaty Establishing the European Community (EC Treaty; Treaty of Rome, originally drawn up 1957)

Directives
Council Directive 76/207/EC of 9 February 1976, on the implementation of the principle of equal treatment for men and women as regards access to employment, vocational training and promotion, and working conditions
Council Directive 97/81/EC of 15 December 1997, concerning the Framework Agreement on part-time work concluded by UNICE, CEEP and the ETUC
Council Directive 99/70/EC of 28 June 1999, concerning the framework agreement on fixed-term work concluded by ETUC, UNICE and CEEP
Council Directive 2000/43/EC of 29 June 2000, implementing the principle of equal treatment between persons irrespective of racial or ethnic origin
Council Directive 2000/78/EC of 27 November 2000, establishing a general framework for combating discrimination on the grounds of religion or belief, disability, age or sexual orientation as regards employment and occupation, with a view to putting into effect in the member states the principle of equal treatment

154   Bibliography

Council of Europe

Conventions
Convention on Human Rights and Biomedicine (ETS no. 164)

Recommendations
Recommendation No. R (92) 3 on Genetic Testing and Screening for Health
    Care Purposes

National legislation

Denmark

Lovbekendtgørelse 1986-10-24 nr 726 om forsikringsaftaler (Proclamation of
    Law on Insurance Contracts)
Lov nr 286 af 24 April 1996 om brug af helbredsoplysninger mv på arbejds-
    markedet (Act concerning the use of health information, etc., in the labour
    market)
Bekendtgørelse nr 777 af 17/08/2000 af lov om tilsyn med firmapensionskasser
    (Proclamation on the Act on supervision of corporate pension funds)

Norway

Lov av 5 august 1994 nr 56 om medisinsk bruk av bioteknologi (Act on the
    medical use of biotechnology)

Sweden

Försäkringsavtalslag (1927:77) (Insurance Contracts Act)

Official publications

European Community

Proposal for a council directive establishing a general framework for equal treat-
    ment in employment and occupation (COM/99/0565)
Proposal for a council directive implementing the principle of equal treatment
    between persons irrespective of racial or ethnic origin (COM/99/0566)

Council of Europe

Explanatory Report (1996), Convention on Human Rights and Biomedicine
    (ETS no. 164)

Denmark

Government bills

Folketingstidende, 1996–97, tillægg A, p. 3472 ff. (Ftl vedr forsikringsaftalet mv) (Insurance contracts etc.)

Norway

Government bills

Ot prp nr 49 (1988/89), Lov om forsikringsavteler (Act on insurance contracts)

Other legislation in preparation

NOU 1991:6, Mennesker og bioteknologi (Human beings and biotechnology)

NOU 2000:23, Forsikringssepskapers innhemting, bruk og lagring av helseopplysninger (On the obtaining, use and storing of information on personal health by insurance companies)

Sweden

Government bills

Prop 1997/98:177, Ny lag om åtgärder mot etnisk diskriminering i arbetslivet (New act on measures against discrimination in working life)

Prop 2001/02:49, Senareläggning av premiepensionens efterlevandeskydd fore pensionstiden (Postponement of survivors' protection before retirement age under the premium pension system)

Other legislation in preparation

SOU 1925:21, Förslag till lag om försäkringsavtal m.m. (Proposal for an Act on insurance contracts etc.)

SOU 1995:5, Vårdens svåra val (The difficult choice facing health services)

Ds 1996:13, Genetisk integritet – vem har rätt att använda information från genetiska undersökningar? (Genetic privacy: who has the right to use information from genetic investigations?)

Skr 1998/99:136, Genetisk integritet (Genetic privacy)

Books and articles

Akerlof, G. (1970), 'The Market for Lemons: Quality Uncertainty and the Market Mechanism', *Quarterly Journal of Economics*, 84, 488

Altenstetter, C. (1986), 'German Social Security Programs: An Interpretation of Their Development', in D. E. Ashford and E. W. Kelley (eds.), *Nationalizing Social Security in Europe and America*, Greenwich, CT: JAI Press, 79

Arrow, K. J. (1963), 'Uncertainty and the Welfare Economics of Medical Care', *American Economic Review*, 53, 941

Arthur, J., and W. Shaw (eds.) (1991), *Justice and Economic Distribution*, New Jersey: Prentice-Hall

Ashford, D. E. (1986), 'Introduction to Part I', in D. E. Ashford and E. W. Kelley (eds.), *Nationalizing Social Security in Europe and America*, Greenwich, CT: JAI Press

Association of British Insurers (2002), www.abi.org.uk, 25 Feb.

Atiyah, P. S. (1979), *The Rise and Fall of Freedom of Contract*, Oxford: Clarendon Press

Atiyah, P. S. (1989), *Freedom of Contract and the New Right*, Stockholm: Juristförlaget

Atiyah, P. S. (1995), *An Introduction to the Law of Contract*, 5th edn, Oxford: Clarendon Press

Banton, M. (1994), *Discrimination*, Buckingham/Philadelphia: Open University Press

Barr, N. (1992), 'Economic Theory and the Welfare State: A Survey and Interpretation', *Journal of Economic Literature*, 30, 741

Beauchamp, T. L., and J. F. Childress (2001), *Principles of Biomedical Ethics*, 5th edn, New York: Oxford University Press

Bentham, J. (1982 [1789]), *An Introduction to the Principles of Morals and Legislation*, ed. J. H. Burns and D. L. A. Hart, London: Methuen

Berge, A. (1995), *Medborgarrätt och egenansvar – De sociala försäkringarna i Sverige 1901–1935 (Civil rights and personal responsibility: social insurance in Sweden, 1901–1935)*, Lund: Arkiv Förlag

Bergström, C. F. (1997), 'Presentation av det nya Europafördraget' (Presentation of the new EC Treaty), *Juridisk Tidskrift*, 1997–98, 305

Berlin, I. (1958), *Two Concepts of Liberty*, Oxford: Clarendon Press

Bernitz, U., and A. Kjellgren (1999), *Europarättens grunder (The foundations of European law)*, Stockholm: Norstedts Juridik

Billings, P., M. A. Kohn, M. de Cuevas, J. Beckwith, J. S. Alper and M. R. Natowicz (1992), 'Discrimination as a Consequence of Genetic Testing', *American Journal of Human Genetics*, 50, 476

Bodie, Z. (1990), 'Pensions as Retirement Income Insurance', *Journal of Economic Literature*, 28, 28

Bogdandy, A. von (2000), 'The European Union as a Human Rights Organization? Human Rights and the Core of the European Union', *Common Market Law Review*, 37, 1307

Borna, S., and S. Avila (1999), 'Genetic Information: Consumers' Right to Privacy Versus Insurance Companies' Right to Know: a Public Opinion Survey', *Journal of Business Ethics*, 19, 4, 355

Briggs, A. (1961), 'The Welfare State in Historical Perspective', *European Journal of Sociology*, 2, 221

Brom, M. E. (1991), 'Insurers and Genetic Testing: Shopping for that Perfect Pair of Genes', *Drake Law Review*, 40, 121

Buchanan, A., D. W. Brock, N. Daniels and D. Winkler (2000), *From Chance to Choice – Genetics and Justice*, Cambridge: Cambridge University Press

Capron, A. M. (2000), 'Genetics and Insurance: Accessing and Using Private Information', *Social Philosophy and Policy*, 17, 235

Chadwick, R., and C. Ngwena (1995), 'The Human Genome Project, Predictive Testing and Insurance Contracts: Ethical and Legal Responses', *Res Publica*, 1, 115

Clayton, R., and H. Tomlinson (2000), *The Law of Human Rights*, Oxford/New York: Oxford University Press

Clifford, K. A., and R. P. Iuculano (1987), 'AIDS and Insurance: The Rationale for AIDS-Related Testing', *Harvard Law Review*, 100, 1806

Cohen, G. A. (1986), 'Selfownership, Worldownership and Equality', in F. Lucash (ed.), *Justice and Equality Here and Now*, New York: Cornell University Press, 108

Collins English Dictionary (1998), Millennium Edition, Glasgow: HarperCollins

Collste, G. (1997), 'Personlig integritet' (Personal privacy), in *Integritet, offentlighet och informationsteknik (Privacy, the public domain and information technology)*, SOU 1997:39 (appendix 4), 785

Connor, M., and M. Ferguson-Smith (1997), *Essential Medical Genetics*, Oxford: Blackwell

Danelius, H. (1993), *Mänskliga rättigheter (Human rights)*, 5th edn, Stockholm: Norstedts

Daniels, N. (1990), 'Insurability and the HIV Epidemic: Ethical Issues in Underwriting', *The Milbank Quarterly*, 68, 497

Dawson, W. H. (1973 [1890]), *Bismarck and State Socialism*, New York: Howard Fertig

Diamond, J. (1999), *Guns, Germs and Steel – The Fates of Human Societies*, New York: Norton

Dworkin, G. (1988), *The Theory and Practice of Autonomy*, Cambridge/New York: Cambridge University Press

Dworkin, R. (1977), *Taking Rights Seriously*, London: Duckworth

Dworkin, R. (1985), *A Matter of Principle*, Cambridge, MA: Harvard University Press

The Economist (2000), 'A Survey of Globalisation and Tax', 29 Jan.

The Economist (2002a), 'The Great Cloning Debate', 11 May, 45

The Economist (2002b), 'Gambling', 31 Aug. 26

The Economist (2002c), 'Squeezing the Gnomes', 5 Oct. 86

Eklund, K. (1998), *Jakten på den försvinnande skatten (In pursuit of the disappearing taxes)*, Stockholm: SNS förlag

Financial Times (2001), 18 July

Financial Times (2002), 7 Oct.

Fisher, D. (2001), *Mänskliga rättigheter. En introduktion (Human rights: an introduction)*, Stockholm: Norstedts Juridik

Flood, G. (1999), 'Genteknik och försäkring' (Genetic technology and insurance), *Svensk Försäkring Årsbok (Swedish Insurance Yearbook)*, Stockholm: Svenska Försäkringsföreningen, 105

Flynn, L. (1999), 'The Implications of Article 13 EC – After Amsterdam, Will Some Forms of Discrimination be More Equal Than Others?', *Common Market Law Review*, 36, 1127

Fotheringham, M. (1999), 'Insurers and Genetic Testing: an Uncertain Future', *Insurance Law Journal*, 11, 1

Gauthier, D. (1986), *Morals by Agreement*, Oxford: Clarendon Press

Geller, L. N., J. S. Alper, P. R. Billings, C. I. Barash, J. Beckwith and M. R. Natowicz (1996), 'Individual, Family, and Societal Dimensions of Genetic Discrimination: A Case Study Analysis', *Science and Engineering Ethics*, 2, 71

Glover, J. (1977), *Causing Death and Saving Lives*, Harmondsworth: Penguin

Glover, J. (1984), *What Sort of People Should There Be? Genetic Engineering, Brain Control and their Impact on our Future*, Harmondsworth: Penguin

Gordon, M. (1988), *Social Security Policies in Industrialized Countries: A Comparative Analysis*, New York: Cambridge University Press

Göring, H. H., J. D. Terwilliger and J. Blangero (2001), 'Large Upward Bias in Estimation of Locus-Specific Effects from Genomewide Scans', *American Journal of Human Genetics*, 6, 1357

Gostin, L. (1991), 'Genetic Discrimination: The Use of Genetically Based Diagnosis and Prognosis Tests by Employers and Insurers', *American Journal of Law and Medicine*, 17, 109

Göteborgsposten (2001), 20 Oct.

Hansson, I., C. H. Lyttkens and G. Skogh (1984), 'The Excess Burden of Public Insurance. Some Results from Swedish Data', *International Review of Law and Economics*, 4, 23

Hare, R. (1981), *Moral Thinking*, Oxford: Oxford University Press

Hare, R. (1991), 'Justice and Equality', in J. Arthur and W. Shaw (eds.), *Justice and Economic Distribution*, Englewood Cliffs, NJ: Prentice Hall, 118

Harper, P. (1993), 'Insurance and Genetic Testing', *The Lancet*, 341, 224

Harris, J. (1998), *Clones, Genes, and Immortality: Ethics and the Genetic Revolution*, Oxford: Oxford University Press

Harsanyi, J. (1977), *Rational Behavior and Bargaining Equilibrium in Games and Social Situations*, Cambridge: Cambridge University Press

Hart, H. L. A. (1961), *The Concept of Law*, Oxford: Clarendon Law Series

Hedgecoe, A. (1996), 'Genetic Catch-22: Testing, Risk and Private Health Insurance', *Business & Professional Ethics Journal*, 15, 69

Helgesson, P. (2001), 'DNA-chips på löpande band' (DNA chips off the assembly line), *Dagens nyheter*, 13 Nov.

Hellner, J. (1994), *Rättsteori (Theory of law)*, 2nd edn, Stockholm: Juristförlaget

Hellner, J. (2001), *Metodproblem i rättsvetenskapen (Methodological problems in jurisprudence)*, Stockholm: Jure

Hertzman, O. (1996), 'Social välfärd genom privat försäkring' (Social welfare by private insurance), in Dufwa, B., A. Kleverman, R.-M. Lundström and E. Tidefelt (eds.), *Vänbok till Erland Strömbäck (Esseys in Honor of Erland Strömbäck)*, Stockholm: Svenska Försäkringsföreningen, 193

Holm, S. (1999), 'There Is Nothing Special about Genetic Information', in A. Tompson and R. Chadwick (eds.), *Genetic Information: Acquisition, Access and Control*, New York: Kluwer Academics/Plenum Publishers, 97

Holtug, N. (1999), 'Genetic Knowledge in a Just Society', in A. Tompson and R. Chadwick (eds.), *Genetic Information: Acquisition, Access and Control*, New York: Kluwer Academics/Plenum Publishers, 283

Husted, J. (1997), 'Autonomy and a Right not to Know', in R. Chadwick, M. Levitt and D. Shickle (eds.), *The Right to Know and the Right not to Know*, Aldershot: Ashgate, 55

Inman, R. P. (1987), 'Markets, Governments and the "New" Political Economy', in A. J. Auerbach and M. Feldstein, *Handbook of Public Economics*, II, Amsterdam: Elsevier Science Publishers

Insurance in Europe, 1996, 25; 1999, p. 11, Brussels: Eurostat DG15

Isaksson, A. (2001), 'Enkla problem, enkla lösningar' (Simple problems, simple answers), *Dagens Industri*, 21 Dec.

Johnston, M. (1999), 'Selling Souls: Ethical Theory and the Commercialisation of Genetic Information', in A. Tompson and R. Chadwick (eds.), *Genetic Information: Acquisition, Access and Control*, New York: Kluwer Academics/Plenum Publishers, 79

Junestav, M. (2001), 'Arbetslinjen i den svenska socialförsäkringsdebatten och lagstiftningen 1930–1955' (The work first principle in the Swedish social insurance debate and legislation, 1930–1955), licentiate dissertation, Uppsala University

Kant, I. (1996 [1785]), 'Groundwork of the Metaphysics of Morals', in *The Cambridge Edition of the Works of Immanuel Kant: Practical Philosophy*, ed. M. J. Gregor, Cambridge: Cambridge University Press

Kass, N. E. (1997), 'Genetic Testing for Health and Life Insurance', in M. A. Rothstein (ed.), *Genetic Secrets: Protecting Privacy and Confidentiality in the Genetic Era*, New Haven: Yale University Press

Kotlikoff, L. J. (1996), 'Privatization of Social Security: How it Works and Why it Matters', in J. M. Poterba (ed.), *Tax Policy and the Economy*, NBER, Cambridge, MA: MIT Press, 1

Kristofferson, U. (2000), 'Kommer genetiken att revolutionera sjukvården? Skepsis mot överdrivna förväntningar' (Will genetic technology revolutionise health care? Scepticism in the face of exaggerated expectations), *Läkartidningen*, 47, 5499

Krueger, A. B. (2000), 'From Bismarck to Maastricht: The March to European Union and the Labor Compact', *Labour Economics*, 7, 117

Kymlicka, W. (1990), *Contemporary Political Philosophy*, New York: Oxford University Press

Launis, V. (2000), 'The Use of Genetic Test Information in Insurance: The Argument from Indistinguishability Reconsidered', *Science and Engineering Ethics*, 6, 299

Lemmens, T. (1999), 'Private Parties, Public Duties?: The Shifting Role of Insurance Companies in the Genetic Era', in A. Tompson and R. Chadwick (eds.), *Genetic Information: Acquisition, Access and Control*, New York: Kluwer Academics/Plenum Publishers, 31

Lemmens, T. (2000), 'Selective Justice, Genetic Discrimination, and Insurance: Should We Single Out Genes in Our Laws?', *McGill Law Journal*, 45, 347

Lemmens, T., and P. Bahamin (1998), 'Genetics in Life, Disability and Additional Health Insurance in Canada: A Comparative Legal and Ethical Analysis', in B. M. Knoppers (ed.), *Socio-Ethical Issues in Human Genetics*, Cowansville (Québec): Yvon Blais, 115

Lenaerts, K. (2000), 'Fundamental rights in the European Union', *European Law Review*, 25, 575

Lindbeck, A. (1995), 'Hazardous Welfare State Dynamics', *American Economic Review*, 85, 9

Locke, J. (1988 [1689]), *Two Treaties of Government*, ed. P. Laslett, New York: Cambridge University Press

Lundgren, N. G. (1996), 'Trade and Maritime Transport Costs: The Evolution of Global Markets', *Resources Policy*, 22, 5

McGleenan, T. (1997), 'Rights to Know and not to Know: Is There a Need for a Genetic Privacy Law', in R. Chadwick, M. Levitt and D. Shickle (eds.), *The Right to Know and the Right not to Know*, Aldershot: Ashgate, 43

Masson, P. R., and M. Mussa (1995), 'Long-Term Tendencies in Budget Deficits and Debt', *IMF WP/95/128*, Washington DC, 1

Mattsson, D. (2001), 'Genteknik och försäkringar' (Genetic technology and insurance), *Svensk Juristtidning*, 309

Mayer, N. R., K. R. Smith, C. D. Zick and J. R. Botkin (1999), 'Coercion, Control, and Consequence in Genetic Testing: Views on Insurance among Tested Individuals and the General Public', in A. Tompson and R. Chadwick (eds.), *Genetic Information: Acquisition, Access and Control*, New York: Kluwer Academics/Plenum Publishers, 41

Mill, J. S. (1974 [1859]), *On Liberty*, Harmondsworth: Penguin

Mill, J. S. (1962 [1863]), *Utilitarianism*, ed. M. Warnock, London: Collins

Miller, D. (1976), *Social Justice*, Oxford: Clarendon Press

Munthe, C. (1999), *Pure Selection: The Ethics of Preimplantation Genetic Diagnosis and Choosing Children Without Abortion*, Göteborg: Acta Universitatis Gothoburgensis

Nozick, R. (1974), *Anarchy, State and Utopia*, New York: Basic Books

Nybergh, F. (1997), *Avtalsfrihet – rätt till avtal (Freedom of contract: the right to enter into contracts)*, Copenhagen: Nordiska Rådet, (Nord 1997:10)

Nys, H., C. J. Nederveen, H. D. C. Roscam Abbing and J. K. M. Gevers (1993), *Predictive Genetic Information and Life Insurance: Legal Aspects: Towards a European Policy?*, Maastricht: University of Limburg, Department of Health Law

OECD (1983), *Historical Statistics 1960–1981*, Paris

OECD (1998), *Maintaining Prosperity in an Ageing Society*, Paris

OECD (2001), *Historical Statistics 1970–1999*, Paris

OECD (annual, 1993; 2002), *Insurance Statistics Yearbook*, Paris

O'Neill, O. (1998), 'Insurance and Genetics: The Current State of Play', *The Modern Law Review*, 61, 716

Ortner, T. (2001), 'Genteknik och personförsäkring' (Genetic technology and personal insurance), dissertation, Faculty of Law, Lund University

Oxford English Dictionary (1989), 2nd edn, Oxford: Clarendon

Parfit, D. (1984), *Reasons and Persons*, Oxford: Oxford University Press

Parfit, D. (1997), 'Equality and Priority', *Ratio*, 10, 202

Rachels, J. (1991), 'What People Deserve', in J. Arthur, and W. Shaw (eds.) (1991), *Justice and Economic Distribution*, Prentice Hall, NJ: 136

Radetzki, Marcus (1996), 'Premiedifferentiering: effektivitet kontra solidaritet' (Premium differentiation: efficiency versus solidarity), in B. Dufwa *et al.* (eds.), *Vänbok till Erland Strömbäck (Esseys in Honour of Erland Strömbäck)*, Stockholm: Svenska Försäkringsföreningen, 243

Radetzki, Marcus (2001), 'Genteknik och försäkring' (Genetic technology and insurance), *Nordisk Försäkringstidskrift*, 82, 1

Radetzki, Marcus, and Marian Radetzki (2000), 'Private Arrangements to Cover Large-scale Liabilities Caused by Nuclear and Other Industrial Catastrophes', *Geneva Papers on Risk and Insurance, Issues and Practice*, 25, 180

Rasmusson, M. (2001), 'Kan ett långt liv gå i arv?' (Can longevity be inherited?), *Svenska Dagbladet*, 3 Aug.

Rawls, J. (1972), *A Theory of Justice*, Oxford: Clarendon Press

Resnik, M. D. (1997), *Choices: An Introduction to Decision Theory*, 4th edn, Minneapolis: Minnesota University Press

Rhodes, R. (1998), 'Genetic Links, Family Ties and Social Bonds: Rights and Responsibilities in the Face of Genetic Knowledge', *Journal of Medicine and Philosophy*, 23, 10

Rimlinger, G. V. (1971), *Welfare Policy and Industrialization in Europe, America and Russia*, New York: Wiley

Roemer, J. (1995), *Equality or Opportunity: A Theory and Examples*, Davis, CA: University of California, Davis

Rosén, E. (1999), 'Genetic Information and Genetic Discrimination: How Medical Records Vitiate Legal Protection. A Comparative Analysis of International Legislation and Policies', *Scandinavian Journal of Public Health*, 27, 166

Rothstein, M. A. (1997), 'Genetic Secrets: A Policy Framework', in M. A. Rothstein (ed.), *Genetic Secrets: Protecting Privacy and Confidentiality in the Genetic Era*, New Haven: Yale University Press

Rothstein, M. A. (ed.) (1997), *Genetic Secrets: Protecting Privacy and Confidentiality in the Genetic Era*, New Haven: Yale University Press

Royal Social Board (1938), *Social Work and Legislation in Sweden*, Stockholm: Tiden

Samuelson, P. (1967), Leader, *Newsweek*, 13 Feb.

Sandberg, A. (2000), 'Att våga välja' (Daring to choose), www.smedjan.com, 2 Nov.

Sandberg, P. (1995), 'Genetic Information and Life Insurance: A Proposal for an Ethical European Policy', *Social Sciences and Medicine*, 40, 1549

Sandberg, P. (1996), 'Genetic Information and Life Insurance: A Proposal for an Ethical European Policy', Ph.D. dissertation, Norwegian University of Science and Technology

Schatz, B. (1987), 'The AIDS Insurance Crisis: Underwriting or Overreaching?', *Harvard Law Review*, 100, 1782

Schiek, D. (1999), 'Freedom of Contract and a Non-Discrimination Principle – Irreconcilable Antonyms', in T. Loenen and P. R. Rodrigues (eds.), *Non-Discrimination Law: Comparative Perspectives*, The Hague/London/Boston: Kluwer Law International, 77

Selmer, K. S. (1990), *Forsikringsavtaleloven med forarbeider (The Insurance Contracts Act and its preparation)*, Oslo: Tano

Silver, L. M. (1997), *Remaking Eden, Cloning and Beyond in a Brave New World*, New York: Avon Books

Smith, K. R., C. D. Zick, N. R. Smith and J. R. Botkin (1999), 'Genetic Testing and Adverse Selection in the Market for Life Insurance', in A. Tompson and R. Chadwick (eds.), *Genetic Information: Acquisition, Access and Control*, New York: Kluwer Academics/Plenum Publishers, 57

Söderström, L., F. Andersson, P. G. Edebalk and A. Kruse (2001), *Privatiseringens gränser – Perspektiv på Välfärdspolitiken (The limits of privatisation: perspectives on welfare policies)*, Stockholm: Välfärdspolitiska Rådets Rapport 2000, SNS förlag

Steiner, H. (1997), 'Choice and Circumstance', *Ratio*, 10, 296

Strömholm, S. (1996), *Rätt, rättskällor och rättstillämpning (Law, sources of law and application of the law)*, 5th edn, Stockholm: Norstedts Juridik

Takala, T. (2000), *Genes, Sense and Sensibility: Philosophical Studies on the Ethics of Modern Biotechnologies*, Reports from the Department of Philosophy, Helsinki: University of Turku

Tännsjö, T. (1998), *Hedonistic Utilitarianism*, Edinburgh: Edinburgh University Press

Tännsjö, T. (1999), *Coercive Care: The Ethics of Choice in Health and Medicine*, London/New York: Routledge

Tanzi, V. (2001), 'Globalization and the Work of Fiscal Termites', *Finance & Development*, 38, 34

Tanzi, V., and L. Schuknecht (1995), 'The Growth of Government and the Reform of the State in Industrial Countries', *IMF WP/95/130*, Washington DC, 1

Teune, H. (1986), 'The Political Development of the Welfare State in the United States', in D. E. Ashford and E. W. Kelley (eds.), *Nationalizing Social Security in Europe and America*, Greenwich, CT: JAI Press, 22

Titmus, R. M. (1950), *Problems of Social Policy*, London: Longman, Green

Wachbroit, R. (1988), 'Making the Grade: Testing for Human Genetic Disorders', *Hofstra Law Review*, 16, 583

Wahlström J. (2002), 'Folkets oro är befogad' (People are right to be worried), *Dagens Nyheter*, 19 Feb.

Waltzer M. (1983), *Spheres of Justice: A Defence of Pluralism and Equality*, Oxford: Blackwell

Weaver, C. L. (1982), *The Crisis in Social Security – Economic and Political Origins*, Durham, NC: Duke University Press

Weissbrodt, D. (1988), 'Human Rights: a Historical Perspective', in P. Davies (ed.), *Human Rights*, London/New York: Routledge, 1

Williams, B. (1973), 'A Critique of Utilitarianism', in J. J. C. Smart and B. Williams, *Utilitarianism: For and Against*, Cambridge: Cambridge University Press

Wilson, A., and G. S. MacKay (1941), *Old Age Pensions; An Historical and Critical Study*, London: Oxford University Press

Wolf, S. (1995), 'Beyond Genetic Discrimination: Towards the Broader Harm of Geneticism', *Journal of Law, Medicine and Ethics*, 23, 345

World Bank (1994), *Averting the Old Age Crisis*, Oxford: Oxford University Press

World Bank (1995), *World Development Report*, Washington DC

World Bank (1999), *World Development Indicators*, Washington DC

World Bank (2000a), *World Development Report*, Washington DC

World Bank (2000b), *World Development Indicators*, Washington DC

Wortham, L. (1986), 'Insurance Classifications: Too Important to Be Left to Actuaries', *University of Michigan Journal of Law Reform*, 19, 349

Young, I. M. (1990), *Justice and the Politics of Difference*, Princeton: Princeton University Press

Index